E-mail Messages from our Viewers

I love the show! Jeff and the whole crew make me laugh and there are wonderful recipes to try. Dan's desserts are usually very simple, but elegant. . .

Katie
Chino, CA

Love your show . . it's presented with wild abandonment. The recipes are very down-to-earth and easy to assemble, not to mention delicious.

Trudie
Redlands, CA

Both of my kids love to sit and watch you cook. Your recipes are outstanding and always look sooo good. Thanks for showing all of us that it's fun to be in the kitchen.

Debbee
Murietta, CA

The recipes are great – I gained 500 pounds and broke my Bowflex. . .

Jim
Claremont, CA

We like the casualness of it. . we made a few of the recipes and they are a hit. Thanks for the fun and keep it up.

Rod
Yucaipa, CA

You and your staff are so hilarious! Honestly . . I learn the easiest and quickest recipes . . they are simple and to the point

Richard
Rancho Cucamonga

Watching your show helped me get a job today. .I was told on this interview to sell enchiladas to a customer. . .you had just made them on your show, I just repeated all the stuff you said . . .

Nancy
Los Alamitos

Really enjoy the show. Good humor and food. A refreshing change from the normal type of cooking show.

Rick
Fontana

I can't even boil water, but I'm very interested in watching the show. Jeff is very entertaining and talks in a very non-condescending manner, making me believe I can cook too. .

Jim
Anaheim, CA

Printed in the United States of America

ISBN: 0-9743018-0-9

Man in the Kitchen
Jeff and Donna Baker
3233 Grand Avenue #N-191
Chino Hills, CA 91709
www.maninthekitchen.com

Cover photograph by Jerry Laursen

Man in the Kitchen

Recipes from Nine Years of Television

Jeff Baker

Dedicated to the women behind the Man in the Kitchen:

My mother Beverly Baker, who's life illustrated to me that any dream could be realized.

My wife Donna Baker, my partner and soul mate. She encourages me to follow my dreams, and is always there to support me.

My mother-in-law Shari Underwood. She's always been gracious with her time, energy, and support.

My daughter Jill, her delightful sense of humor and optimistic outlook on life provides me with a continual source of inspiration.

Contents

Why These Recipes?

These recipes were included because they, in my opinion, will get you excited about cooking, AND are simple to prepare.

As a kid attempting to get through my boring summer, I wound up in the kitchen, hungry or not, looking for recipes. I was limited by whatever food was in the fridge or cupboard. This was typically frustrating because I'd find the perfect recipe and start piling ingredients on the counter, only to find I was missing ONE key ingredient!

Without that ingredient the recipe was worthless, so I'd return the items to the cupboard and go back to watching Gilligan's Island.

Now, I'm older and can drive to the store, yet I get really ticked off when the store does not have an ingredient needed for my perfect recipe! That's why nearly every recipe in this book will have ingredients you can find at your local grocery store.

The kitchen is the most joyful room in the house. Think about it. The last time you had people over, where did most of them end up?

Nothing makes me happier than firing up the stove, pouring a glass of wine and chatting with friends and/or family as I hover over my stove. My wife Donna and I have some of the best times together in the kitchen, cooking and dreaming about life.

Recipes are like friends. When you find a good one, you hold on tight. Take a minute right now and think about some of your best friends (don't worry; you didn't buy a self-help book). Now, try to remember the day your friendship really began. Where were you?

Chances are, you chose to take an extra step in getting to know that person. That choice resulted in the first steps of your relationship.

Trying new recipes should be viewed the same way. Try a new recipe as often as you can. Before long, one or two will be added to your all-time favorites.

The recipes in this book were featured on our TV show during its first nine years. Each recipe was scrutinized before being featured on the show. The recipe had to taste remarkably good, its ingredients had to be readily accessible, and preparation could not be too complex.

1

With this formula (and a promise to our viewers that cooking would result in ego-satisfying adoration) we felt we had the makings of a pretty decent cooking show. We concluded that guys watching our show would move off their couch and into their kitchen. As our show became more popular, people started recognizing me around town. You can imagine the joy I felt when guys approached me and actually thanked me for inspiring them to cook!

We've attempted to make this book as useful as possible.

The lunch recipes were designed from a need to feed. For example, how many times do you have out-of-town guests visit? What about lunch? Do you give into temptation to go out? That's not always the best idea. You might end up footing the bill each time and that cost adds up. Besides, going out for lunch typically means fatty, sodium ridden fast food. Worst of all – boring! Save your money. Enjoy lunch at home. The lunch recipes in this book were featured because they are interesting, filling, tasty, and best of all – easy!

We've included the mainstay of our show – main course dishes. With these you'll find cures for middle-of-the-week dinner doldrums. Why use leftover roast beef for ordinary stew when you can make Beef Stroganoff or Orange Beef Burritos? Why waste good leftover salmon when you can use it in an exotic carbonara pasta dish?

You'll find an ample inventory of great tasting, main course dinners that everyone will love. And they won't take all afternoon to prepare.

You'll notice a chapter called *Really Impressive Main Entrees*. We wanted to dedicate a chapter to dinners that are a little more exotic than the other main entrees. Prepare these dishes when you wish to generate an "oooohhh" or "ahhhhh" from your guests. They'll adore you and wonder what other hidden talents you possess.

I'd like to discuss romance now. It's a topic most guys avoid because, quite frankly, romance is a hassle, right? Wrong. I've talked to many women about this subject and learned that they don't demand much when it comes to romance. Women will respect any attempt by a guy to be romantic. If we are doing our best, it will be appreciated. A nice dinner prepared by you will mean everything. Take the time to plan. Set the table, open a bottle of decent wine, put on some music, and serve her a romantic meal.

About desserts. Dan Underwood first appeared on our show as a wine expert. His years of experience working for a specialty retailer provided him with a lot of knowledge about wines. Viewers from the early years may remember him as "Dan the Wine Man". He'd visit us occasionally and recommend wines that would compliment the recipe we were featuring.

One day, Dan asked if he could prepare one of his favorite recipes on the show. Donna and I thought this might be an interesting change. Dan prepared his infamous *Fudgy Wudgy Brownies* during the last five minutes of the show. When the show aired, we had so many requests from that recipe; we decided to let Dan make desserts from that point forward.

You'll also find some great appetizers in this book. So great, you might enjoy them as a main course! Live like the French once and awhile; eat smaller portions of richer foods. Remember, moderation is the key to enjoying life.

Our side dishes were designed to be independent, in other words, when we featured them on the show, they did not have to "rely" on the main course. You'll find that our side dishes go with just about anything.

The index of this book has been designed for you to find recipes easily. The recipes have been alphabetized by the main ingredient, or the most notable feature. This concept was viewer-inspired. We found that most viewers didn't remember the exact title of the dish, but could identify a key ingredient.

It's a pleasure to share these recipes with you. I hope reading this book will inspire you to get into your kitchen more often. Be sure to grab a friend or family member and take them with you (chances are, they'll be willing to go). I truly hope that you will experience the same joy I have in my kitchen.

Nine Years of Television

If you are ready to get cooking, flip ahead in this book and find your recipe. If you want to learn more about the history of our show, then read on . . .

Having your own television cooking show is every bit as cool as you might imagine. It's the most fun I've had since playing guitar in a garage band in high school. Imagine if you were able to star in your own TV show about your favorite hobby. Wouldn't you be having fun too?

We started *Man in the Kitchen* as a public access effort using the facilities of our local cable company. I'd read about public access television years earlier, and always wanted to give it a try, but thought it was only available in larger cities. When I found out our little suburban town offered it, I jumped at the chance.

I simply needed an idea for a show. My wife Donna suggested cooking. I liked that, but didn't want to produce an ordinary cooking show. I needed an angle, something different. That's when we decided to aim the show at guys. My goal was to get guys out of the garage and into the kitchen. After all, there were just as many gadgets, if not more, in the kitchen compared to the garage.

Our first few shows were shot in our kitchen at home. Donna and I enlisted the help of friends and family. None of us knew how to work the equipment. We had to figure out everything as we went along. It took us a full holiday weekend to shoot our first show.

I learned to edit the same way I learned how to ride a bike – trial and error. I brought the raw video footage to the studio and spent hours attempting to make it look like a real TV show. Thankfully, the cable company employed a full-time staff person to help me. I learned a lot from the various people that held this position.

Our first show was cablecast in January of 1995. A bunch of us gathered at our house to watch our creation on the local channel. We'd called the local paper earlier in the week and explained how our new show intended to teach guys how to cook. They liked the premise and featured an article about our show's "premiere". The paper asked me for a publicity photo. I didn't have one, so Donna grabbed a camera and snapped a shot of me in our kitchen holding a pizza. The paper printed it (that same photo ran for over five years above my column in the monthly article I wrote for a local magazine).

The atmosphere in our living room was exciting on the big night. As people chatted around me, my eyes remained nervously glued to the TV as I waited for our show to begin. Our local channel was very typical, most of the day, between local shows, this channel played soft rock and displayed computer generated bulletin boards promoting local events. I was reading about a church bake sale when the music suddenly stopped and the screen went black. The room fell quiet.

A few seconds later, our show started. The room exploded with screams and applause. I can't remember feeling excitement like that (well, maybe when my car won first place in the pinewood derby in third grade). I felt like a rock star. This was my 28 minutes of fame.

Like most TV shows, ours had a 30-second open introducing the show. In ours I walked carefully into the kitchen carrying an orange tool box. When I open the box, instead of pulling out tools, I pull out wooden spoons and spatulas. It was corny, but got the point across. The title of the show was keyed in front of me: *Man in the Kitchen!* (Eventually we removed the exclamation mark.)

We got a lot of positive response from that first show. We decided to produce another one, then another one. We ended up producing about a dozen shows over the next two years.

As we continued to produce shows, our quality improved. We felt confident that our show was ready for a larger audience. I approached Don Leiffer, the program director at PBS affiliate KVCR-TV in San Bernardino. In January of 2000, he added the show to their schedule. This was exciting for us – our little cable show would now be on broadcast television! In January of 2000, our potential viewers grew from 20,000 households to over one million.

When your show is broadcast, it gets to be published in local listings. Each month we submitted a short description of the show to an agency in New York which made the listings available to the published media – typically local newspapers and periodicals like *TV Guide*. I remember standing in line at the grocery store and thumbing through the first *TV Guide* in which our show was listed. That was exciting! There it was, listed at 7:30pm on Thursday nights, up against *Wheel of Fortune*. That's when I felt like *Man in the Kitchen* was a real TV show.

We did everything with essentially no budget. Most people would be surprised at how much equipment was given to us by product sponsors. It's common for companies that produce kitchen equipment to supply public television cooking shows with their products for exposure. Our mixers, food processors, pots, and pans were donated regularly.

This hobby of ours evolved into a routine production with obligations. The cable company was very cooperative about letting us schedule the studio for production of *Man in the Kitchen*. We promised KVCR 26 shows per year. We shot two shows per day. We started shooting in August, and shot every other week until we'd completed 13 shows. We repeated the process in February for our spring schedule.

With a schedule like this, we had to find ways to be efficient. Jim Patrick eventually became the studio manager at the cable company. He suggested we shoot "live to tape". This essentially meant pretending our show was live and barreling through the shoot with minimal stopping. We would only stop if something really disastrous happened – like when something burned, or when I cut my finger (both happened a lot!)

Shooting live to tape proved very efficient. It made it much easier to produce several shows. But more important - we found that shooting like this actually improved the "feel" of the show. Preparing recipes in real time illustrated to the viewer how simple the dish really was. The crew and I had more fun. It seemed like our viewers were actually watching us when we shot.

Once we became a regular show on broadcast TV, reporters from local newspapers and magazines started visiting our set. First time visitors were always amazed to discover that our production was truly a family operation. They seemed even more amazed to see how well we all got along.

The atmosphere on our set was always fun and light – because of the great people that surrounded us. Lee (my father-in-law) operated camera #2, but more importantly was an abundant source of corny jokes. Shari (my mother-in-law), a classic perfectionist, had the crucial job of prepping the food and keeping me organized. Dan (my brother-in-law) and dessert specialist brought his cynical sense of humor to the set. This was the perfect compliment to the dry wit of production assistant Glenn Thornhill (my other brother-in-law).

Our "adopted" family included Greg Wyatt, an irreplaceable person in the production of the show. Greg is remarkable. Many shows might not have been shot because of technical difficulties (inherent with any television production). Greg had a knack for being able to identify problems and fix them, quickly. We were lucky to have him around. He was an exceptional camera operator. I liked having him on the floor during shoots because we had so much fun together.

Another adopted family member was Marit Kams, a truly delightful person who's always a pleasure to be around. As our floor manager, Marit relayed Donna's instructions from the booth out to us on the floor. In this position, Marit would occasionally get in the middle of "friendly" disagreements between Donna and I. Marit was smart enough to know, when in doubt, take Donna's side.

Donna directed the show and kept everybody on schedule. Not all hosts could take direction from wives like this, but I'm really glad I could. She made all the calls regarding camera shots. I credit Donna for the look and feel of the show.

We were blessed to be around such quality people. They created such a natural energy level in the studio. Laughter was abundant. Every shoot was truly a blast.

When the cameras started shooting, this energy level remained. In fact, the crew was always encouraged to participate in the show by making comments in the background. This started one day when Lee blurted out some comment, then the rest of the crew responded to him. I played along - keeping the viewer involved of course. Traditionally, television producers would likely frown at off-camera banter, but we kept doing it. Viewers told us they loved the off-camera banter with the crew. The banter stayed and today remains a regular part of the show.

Eventually, viewers were able to get current show recipes by visiting our web site. It was also a great way for us to get feedback from our viewers. As things progressed with the web site, I'd inevitably get requests from recipes we'd featured the year before (or the year before that). Our resources limited us to the current recipes only. I promised viewers that eventually I'd compile all the recipes in a cookbook. Consider that promise fulfilled.

So far, I've mentioned a handful of people, but I'd like to mention some additional people. Each of these people influenced our show's production, distribution, promotion, or a combination of each:

Chris Little, Jim Murtagh, Kim James, Craig James, Preston Hayslette, Jim Patrick, Les English, Melinda Bitney, Bill Rosendahl, Bill Greene, Tom Bystry, Rusty Townshend, Jerry Laursen, Brian Hannah, Marvin Byrkett, Susan Meyers, Vance Stearns, Raymond Chavez, Tim Abad, Josh Thompson, Diane Schram, Greg Banawitz, Liz Cahn, Barry Fischer, Carla Szczuka, Allan Borgan, David Cohen, Don Hinman, Al Gondos, Lew Warren, Jim Gilbert, Patty Littlejohn , Rick Dulock, Larry Holden, Maura Graber, Claud Beltran, Steve Hammersmith, Gary Brewton, Bob Gonzalas, Ed Beach, Dr. Steve Pulverman, Dr. Hector Costamagna, Frank Salvo, Don Galleano, Will Woods, Shannon Woods, Charles McKee, Kelli Sipp, and Kathy Myers.

My other family members should not go unrecognized. Thanks to my sons Alex and Christian Baker for being patient while I chatted with viewers around town. Thanks to my sisters Barb Lockhart and Carole Nicholas for sharing some great recipes with me. Thanks to my dad Paul Baker for advice about the TV business. Thanks to my late Grandma Marie Baker for letting me hang around the kitchen when she was cooking.

Our kitchen set was built by Rusty Townshend, a viewer from the early days who happened to be a kitchen remodeling contractor. He was instrumental in getting our production into the studio. Subsequently, the set was remodeled by The Great Indoors - thanks to Kelli, Gregory, Kathy, and everybody else there who helped make our kitchen look so wonderful. I'd also like to thank the people at KitchenAid, Le Crueset, Cuisinart, and All-Clad for donating equipment to our set

Special thanks goes out to the local businesses that helped us out over the years including: Hottingers Family Meats, Albertsons, Hobart-Walters, Ralph's/Food 4 Less, Papa Paul/Via Salvo, and Gebhart International.

In addition, I'd like to thank our viewers. Especially those who took the time to send an e-mail message, or approach me with encouraging words. Your support and inspiration kept us going for nine years. It's all about you.

Most importantly, I'd like to thank God for all his blessings.

The first Man in the Kitchen crew. This photo was taken in our kitchen in 1995.
Left to right, Craig James, Kim James, Lori Underwood, Dawn Hannah,
Brian Hannah, Dan Underwood, Helen Frank, Donna Baker.

The first "publicity" photo of Jeff. Taken by Donna in our kitchen.

Friends and family gather for the television debut of Man in the Kitchen, January, 1995.

Les English shoots some footage in the field.

Breakfast
Brunch and Lunch

Stacked Breakfast Enchiladas

Cotija is a Mexican cheese - it's found in the specialty cheese section of most grocery stores. If you can't find it, use grated Jack or cheddar cheese.

- 8 oz Cotija cheese, crumbled
- 1 dozen corn tortillas, blanched in vegetable oil over medium high heat
- 14 oz refried beans
- 6 large eggs
- 2 tbs butter
- ½ cup olives, sliced
- 14 oz red enchilada sauce, heated

Fry eggs in butter to your liking (sunny side up, over easy, etc). Spread one tortilla with refried beans, top with some Cojita cheese. Add another tortilla, then a cooked egg. Top with enchilada sauce, olives, and more Cojita. Serve. Makes 6.

Baja Quiche

- 6 - 8 fresh corn tortillas
- 12 oz. refried beans
- 8 oz. chorizo (fully cooked and drained of excess fat)
- 4 oz. jack cheese, grated
- 2 eggs
- fresh avocado slices
- fresh tomato slices
- fresh cilantro

Preheat oven to 350 degrees. Layer tortillas in a heavy skillet to cover bottom. Spread beans over tortillas, top with cilantro, then cheese. Lightly beat eggs in separate bowl then pour over cheese. Bake for 20 - 30 minutes (until eggs have firmed up and cheese is slightly browned). Garnish with avocado, tomato, and cilantro

Prussian Omelet

Years ago, my mom took me to breakfast at a Greek diner near her home in the Queen Anne Hill district of Seattle. She suggested this omelet. I tried it and immediately became hooked. Years later, I visited several diners in southern California and none of them featured this omelet on their menu. I re-created it from memory and the result was pretty close. Give it a shot!

- 6 large eggs
- water
- peanut oil
- 1 package frozen hash browns, cooked
- 8 oz sour cream
- 1 lb bacon, cooked, drained, and broken into pieces
- 6 green onions, chopped

Makes 3 – 4 omelets: Beat eggs in a bowl. Add 1 teaspoon water halfway through. Add 1 tablespoon peanut oil to an 8" sauté pan that has been preheated over medium heat. Pour enough egg mixture into pan to cover bottom. Cook until semi solid then turn over. Top one side with remaining ingredients (separated). Fold over and slide onto a plate.

Sausage Mushroom Omelet

- 12 eggs
- 2 tbs water
- 4 - 6 oz country style sausage, fully cooked
- 4 oz. mushrooms, sliced and sautéed in butter
- 3 oz. Swiss cheese (or any white cheese), grated
- peanut oil (or vegetable oil)

Pre-heat non-stick omelet pan over medium low heat. Wisk eggs and water together in a bowl or pitcher until well blended. Add oil to pan, when hot pour in just enough egg mixture to cover bottom. Let cook a bit. Use spatula to move eggs slightly and let runny part cook. When omelet appears almost cooked, turn over. Add cooked sausage, mushrooms, and cheese to one side. Fold over and slide onto plate.

Potato Frittata

This tasty frittata is a Christmas morning tradition with Donna's family. It's a great brunch meal for any occasion because you can prepare it the night before.

- ½ cup butter, melted
- 2 cups onions, chopped

Sauté onions in Butter, then add the following

- 2 cups cooked ham or sausage
- 1 ½ tsp ground allspice
- 2 cups mushroom, chopped
- 1 cup spinach, chopped, drained well
- 1 ½ tsp nutmeg

Beat together the following:

- 16 eggs
- 1/2 cup parsley, chopped
- 1 cup cream
- 2 tsp salt

Stir in the following:

- 3 cups (1lb) cheese (preferably Swiss), grated
- 4 cups potato, grated, excess water from potatoes squeezed out

Pour all above into 2 greased 9" x 13" oven proof pan. Bake 35-40 minutes for one pan or 1 hour plus for 2 at 350-375 degrees. If you combine this recipe into one larger pan it will take about 1 to 1 ½ hour to cook. Test with knife to be sure it is done.

17

Eggs Benedict

This recipe was featured in a show in which we encouraged viewers to impress their Mother-in-Law for brunch by preparing brunch. It's easy and so delicious. The secret is using the packaged, Knorr brand Hollandaise sauce. I think it's better than sauce from scratch.

- 8 eggs
- ¼ cup water
- 1 package *Knorr* Hollandaise sauce (requires butter and milk)
- 8 English muffins
- 8 slices Canadian bacon
- dash of paprika
- ground pepper

Make the sauce per package directions, cover to keep warm. Heat a medium sized skillet to medium heat. Melt a tablespoon of the butter, and then crack 4 eggs into the skillet (try not to break yolk). Gently pour the water around the outside of the eggs. Cover and let the eggs steam until yolks appear to be desired doneness. Repeat with remaining eggs.

In the meantime, brown Canadian bacon in another skillet just long enough to heat. Toast English muffins. Place a slice of Canadian bacon on each muffin, followed by an egg, then top with Hollandaise sauce. Sprinkle tops lightly with paprika and ground pepper for taste.

Eggs Arnold

- ¼ cup butter or margarine
- 1 medium onion, sliced thin
- 8 eggs, beaten
- 1 tsp Tabasco sauce
- 1 tbs parsley, chopped
- 4 oz. hard salami, sliced
- 4 oz. Swiss cheese, sliced
- 2 tbs brown mustard
- 6 - 8 English Muffins, toasted
- salt and pepper to taste

Melt butter on heavy skillet over medium heat. Add onions and cook slowly for 15 – 20 minutes. Add eggs and stir until they begin to firm up. Fold in parsley. Spread English muffins with butter, then top with cheese and salami. Spoon cooked eggs over salami and serve.

Peanut Butter and Maple French toast

- 6 slices white bread
- 2 eggs
- ¼ cup milk
- 2 tbs butter
- ½ cup maple syrup
- ½ cup peanut butter
- ¼ cup maple syrup
- ¾ cup vanilla yogurt
- 1 green apple, cored and sliced into eighths
- ½ cup granola

Melt butter over medium low heat in skillet. Combine eggs and milk. Dip bread in egg mixture and fry on both sides until brown.

Mix peanut butter and ½ cup maple syrup in glass bowl. Microwave on high power for one minute. Carefully stir mixture. Combine ½ cup maple syrup and yogurt in another bowl. Cover French toast with peanut butter mixture, followed by yogurt mixture. Top with apples and granola.

Tuscan Eggs Benedict

The following three recipes were featured by Jim and Trish Gordon of Gold Mountain Manor, a beautiful and historic Bed and Breakfast in Big Bear, California. We shot a Mother's Day special up there one year.

- 6 freshly baked Buttermilk Biscuits, cut in half
- 12 slices Canadian bacon
- 12 large eggs, poached (see recommended procedure below)
- ¾ cup artichoke hearts, sliced
- 1 12oz. can stewed tomatoes
- ¼ cup sun dried tomatoes (reserve packing oil)

Sauce

Heat tomatoes in skillet. Add chopped sun dried tomatoes (with some packing oil to taste). Add sliced artichoke hearts. Let simmer for about 20 minutes.

Heat olive oil in medium skillet. Fry bacon only until heated. Place piece of bacon on each biscuit or muffin. Top each biscuit with poached egg. Cover with sauce and serve with Home fries.

Yukon Gold Home fries

- 5 - 6 Gold potatoes
- olive oil

Preheat oven to 450 degrees. Slice potatoes "French fry" style. Place on shallow baking sheet. Drizzle with olive oil. Bake for 20 - 25 minutes. Season with salt.

Croissant French Toast with Caramelized Banana Topping

French toast:

- 6 Croissants (cut in half cross-wise)
- 9 large eggs
- ½ cup milk
- 2 tsp cinnamon
- 2 tsp vanilla

Whisk together eggs – vanilla in a small bowl. Arrange Croissants on a baking sheet or in Pyrex dishes. Pour the egg mixture over and allow to seep in, turning the croissants once. Set aside and make banana topping.

Banana Topping:

- 3 bananas, cut in ½ inch pieces
- ¼ cup brown sugar
- ½ cup maple syrup
- ¼ cup unsalted butter

Melt butter in non-stick sauté pan. Add bananas and brown sugar, sautéing for a couple of minutes. Add maple syrup and allow to cook down until bananas are slightly soft.

Make the French toast by melting butter in non stick pan or griddle over medium high heat. Brown French toast on Both Sides. Smother in bananas.

22

Gingerbread Waffles with Fresh Berry Topping

- 2½ cups all purpose flour
- ¼ cup brown sugar
- 4 tsp baking powder
- 1 tsp baking soda
- 1 tbs each: espresso powder and ground ginger
- 1 tsp each: cinnamon, ground cloves & nutmeg
- ¼ tsp salt (pinch will do)
- 2 eggs
- 1½ cups cultured buttermilk
- ½ cup light molasses, slightly warmed in the microwave (30 seconds in the jar, cap off) for easy mixing
- 6 tbs unsalted butter, melted

Preheat waffle iron to medium high setting. Spray waffle iron with non-stick spray. Combine all dry ingredients in a large bowl. Wisk the eggs, buttermilk, and molasses in a separate small bowl until foamy. Pour over dry ingredients and mix until just combined. Drizzle with melted butter and fold in. Make your topping and let waffles sit for a couple of minutes.

Topping:

- 1 12oz package frozen unsweetened mixed berries, slightly thawed
- 1 pint fresh strawberries or whatever berry is in season (blueberries are great, too)
- 1 ½ tsp cornstarch mixed with ½ cup warm water – should look like milk

Pour partially thawed berries into medium sized saucepan over medium heat. While they break down, cut berries into halves. After frozen berries have partially reduced down, add fresh berries and allow to cook for a few moments. When the berries are a cross between broken down and firm, stir in your corn starch mixture and lower heat.

Make your waffles while the sauce simmers down a little more and serve with a dollop of butter and the berry sauce.

Pecan Waffles with Bananas

Dan Underwood concluded many of our shows with a fine dessert. Some of these desserts could be served for breakfast. Here's one of them.

- 1½ cups sifted flour
- ½ tsp salt
- 1¼ tsp baking powder
- ½ tsp baking soda
- 2 eggs, separated
- 1¼ cups buttermilk
- 4 tbs melted butter
- 4 oz pecans

Finely chop pecans. Toast in dry skillet over medium heat. Set aside.

Sift flour, salt, baking powder and baking soda together. Beat egg yolks and add buttermilk and butter. Add flour and beat with rotary beater until smooth. Stir in pecans. Fold in stiffly beaten egg whites. Bake in hot waffle iron. Top with bananas (see below)

Pecan-Cinnamon Monkey Bread

- 1– 2 loaves prepared frozen bread dough
- 1 cup granulated sugar
- 1 cup brown sugar
- cinnamon to taste
- ½ cup unsalted butter, melted
- ½ cup pecans, chopped

Thaw dough per package directions. Form dough into golf ball size pieces. Mix sugar and cinnamon and put mixture into a bowl. Roll each dough ball in the mixture coating completely. Layer them in a bundt pan coated with vegetable oil. Mix brown sugar, melted butter and nuts. Pour over layers. Bake at 350 degrees for 35 minutes or until done.

Chocolate Pancakes with Chocolate-Raspberry Sauce

- ¼ cup All-purpose flour
- 2 tbs sugar
- 1 ½ tsp unsweetened cocoa powder
- ¼ tsp baking powder
- pinch of salt
- 1 lg egg white
- ¼ cup skim milk
- 1 tsp vegetable oil
- ¼ tsp pure vanilla extract

Chocolate-Raspberry Sauce

- 1/3 cup sugar
- 2 tbs unsweetened cocoa powder
- 3 tbs seedless raspberry jam
- 2 tsp Framboise (optional)
- 1 ½ tsp cornstarch

Chocolate Pancakes

In a medium-sized bowl, stir together flour, sugar, cocoa, baking powder and salt. In a small bowl, whisk together egg white, milk, oil and vanilla. Make a well in the center of the dry ingredients and gradually whisk in the liquid mixture, stirring just until combined. Let the batter stand for 5 minutes, or refrigerate for up to 1 hour. Cook as a normal pancake.

Chocolate-Raspberry Sauce

In a small saucepan, whisk together sugar, cocoa and cornstarch. Gradually whisk in 1/4 c water and jam. Bring to a simmer over medium heat, whisking constantly. Remove from the heat and stir in Framboise if using. Let cool slightly (The sauce can be stored, covered, in the refrigerator for up to 1 week). Place two pancakes on a plate, spoon on Ice cream and then pour some of the sauce over everything and serve.

Poppy seed Bread

We first made this sweet, dense bread on a Holiday show. This recipe has been a family favorite for years. It also makes a perfect gift.

- 3 cups flour
- 1 ½ tsp salt
- 1 ½ tsp baking powder
- 3 eggs
- 1 ½ cups milk
- 1 1/8 cups vegetable oil
- 2 ¼ cups sugar
- 1 ½ tsp poppy seeds
- 1 ½ tsp vanilla
- 1 ½ tsp almond extract
- 1 ½ tsp butter flavoring

Mix all the ingredients together well. And pour into 2 well greased loaf pans, 2/3 full. Baker at 350 degrees for 1 hour.

Give this bread the old toothpick trick to test if done. Put toothpick into the center of the bread and if in comes out clean it's done. Pour glaze over top of hot bread (while still in pan).

Glaze

- 1 ¼ cup orange juice
- ¾ cup powder sugar
- ½ tsp butter flavoring
- 1 ½ tsp vanilla extract
- ½ tsp almond extract

27

Country Fried Steak with Cream Gravy

- 1 lb round steak, ½ inch thick
- 1 cup flour
- 1 tsp baking powder
- ½ tsp baking soda
- ½ tsp ground black pepper
- ½ tsp salt
- 1 cup buttermilk
- 1 egg
- 2 tsp Tabasco sauce
- shortening

Cut steak into 4 equal portions. Place between wax paper and pound well with tenderizing mallet (or side of heavy skillet). Tenderize well. Put flour on plate. In medium bowl, combine baking powder through egg , stir well.

Over medium-high heat, melt enough shortening in heavy, deep skillet to make about 2 – 3 inches deep when melted. Dredge steak in flour until covered. Then dip in buttermilk batter and cover. Return to flour and cover until as dry as possible.

Fry two steaks until bottom is browned, turn over and fry until cooked. Drain steaks on paper towel. Repeat for remaining steaks. Keep warm while preparing gravy.

Gravy:
- 1 cup beef stock, ¼ cup reserved
- 1 tbs flour
- 1 cup evaporated milk
- ½ tsp ground pepper
- salt to taste

Make gravy by draining all but 1/3 cup of the fat in the skillet (leave most of browned batter pieces too). Combine ¼ cup of the beef stock with flour, set aside. Add remaining beef stock and deglaze pan turning heat back up to medium-high and use spatula to scrape bits off bottom of pan. Stir in evaporated milk and bring to slight boil. Add flour/stock mixture slowly to thicken, stirring constantly. When thick, add pepper and salt to taste. Pour gravy over steaks. Serve immediately.

Caramelized-Onion, Spinach, and Ham Quiche

*Quiche has taken a lot of abuse over the years. In reality, it's the perfect
"guy" dish because it's rich, impressive, filling, and best of all – simple to
make. Try making it today, you'll see what I mean.*

- 1 10 oz can refrigerated pie crust, brought to room temperature
- 1 10 oz package frozen spinach, thawed, chopped, and squeezed dry
- ¼ cup sour cream
- 2 tbs shallots, minced
- 1 cup evaporated milk
- ¼ tsp salt
- ¼ tsp pepper
- 2 large egg whites
- 1 large egg
- ¾ cup onions, sliced
- 1/3 cup chopped ham or Canadian bacon
- ¼ cup Monterey Jack cheese, shredded

Place onion slices in a medium skillets with 2 - 3 tablespoons of melted
butter. Sauté onions for 20 - 30 minutes until natural sugars have formed
and browned the onions well.

Preheat oven to 350 degrees. Form dough to fit in 9 inch (oiled) pie pan.
Combine spinach, sour cream and shallots, in a small bowl. Combine
evaporated milk, salt pepper, egg whites, and egg in medium bowl, stir well
with whisk. Stir 1/3 cup milk mixture into spinach mixture, mix. Form into
bottom of pie plate (on top of dough). Add caramelized onions, and then top
with ham and cheese. Pour remaining milk mixture over cheese. Place on
baking sheet 350 degrees for 45 minutes (or until firm). Let stand at least 10
minutes before serving.

Brie and Red Pepper Quiche

- frozen pastry shell, thawed
- 2 tbs butter
- ¾ cup finely chopped sweet red peppers
- ½ lb. Brie, cut in small cubes
- 10 slices bacon, cooked and crumbled
- 3 eggs
- 1 1/3 cup whipping cream
- salt
- cayenne pepper

Preheat oven to 350 degrees. Melt butter in skillet over medium heat. Add peppers and sauté until softened, add to pie crust. Top with Brie and bacon. In bowl, beat eggs and cream. Season with salt and cayenne pepper to taste. Pour over Brie. Bake at 350 degrees for 30 - 40 minutes or until firm. Let set for 10 minutes before serving.

Chicken and Grape Sandwich

The perfect summer sandwich. Bite into this any time of year and the sun will shine!

- 2 tbs celery, chopped
- ½ cup mayonnaise
- 2 tbs lemon juice
- 1/8 tsp onion powder
- 1/8 tsp garlic powder
- 1/8 tsp dried thyme
- 1/8 tsp ground black pepper
- 2 ½ cups chicken breast, cooked
- 1 ½ cups seedless green grapes, halved
- white bread, sliced

Mix together first seven ingredients. Add chicken and grapes. Serve between bread slices.

Orange Chicken Sandwich

- 2 boneless, skinless chicken breasts
- 2 tbs butter, melted
- 2 medium tomatoes, sliced
- 1 avocado, peeled and sliced
- romaine lettuce leaves
- salt and pepper to taste
- sliced sourdough bread

Spread:

- ½ cup mayonnaise
- 2 tbs orange juice concentrate, thawed
- juice of one lime
- ½ tsp ground cumin
- ½ tsp hot sauce

In a small bowl combine all ingredients for the spread and mix well. Season chicken with salt and pepper. Melt butter in skillet over medium heat. Add chicken and cook 5 minutes per side. Reduce heat and let chicken cook until done. Remove and cut chicken across grain into slices. Place on bread slice. Top with spread, and rest of ingredients.

Chicken Sandwich with a Citrus Mayonnaise

Citrus Mayo

- 1/3 cup mayonnaise
- 2 tbs thawed orange juice concentrate
- 1 juice of a lime
- ½ tsp ground cumin
- 1/8 tsp hot sauce

In a small bowl combined the above ingredients and mix.

Sandwich

- 2-3 skinned, boned chicken breast
- ¼ tsp salt
- 1/8 tsp pepper
- cooking spray
- 8 slices of sourdough bread, toasted
- 4 leaves of lettuce
- 2 Roma tomatoes, sliced
- 1 peeled avocado, cut into 8 wedges

Sprinkle salt and pepper on chicken. Place in a large skillet that has been coated with cooking spray. Cook over medium heat for 8 minutes on each side, until done. Cut chicken into strips. Spread citrus Mayonnaise on bread. Place one lettuce leaf of bread then chicken, tomatoes and avocado wedges. Top with other slice of bread.

Chicken and Brie Sandwich with Marinated Tomatoes

<u>Marinated Tomatoes</u>

- ½ cup olive oil
- 2 cups sliced Roma tomatoes
- 2 cloves garlic, diced
- ½ tsp pepper
- ½ tsp salt
- 1 tbs thyme
- 1 tbs balsamic vinegar

Mix together in a small bowl or large plastic zip lock bag. Chill

<u>Sandwich</u>

- ¼ cup mayonnaise
- 1 tbs Dijon mustard
- 1 lg loaf of French bread
- 3 oz Brie cheese, sliced
- 3 cups chicken breast, cooked and shredded
- 2 tsp olive oil
- 1/8 tsp salt
- 2 cups spinach

In a small bowl combine mayonnaise, Dijon mustard and garlic. Spread over top half of bread slice. Spread bottom half of bread with tomato mixture. Place Brie slices over tomatos, then top with chicken and then spinach. Finish with top slice of bread.

Roast Beef Sandwich with Chipotle Mayonnaise

The secret to this excellent sandwich is the mayonnaise you make from scratch – it's easy with a blender or food processor. .

<u>Chipotle Mayonnaise</u>

- 3 egg whites
- 1 – 2 tbs Chipotle
- 1 tbs olive oil

Mix the above ingredients in a small bowl.

<u>Sandwich</u>

- 4 slices of rye bread
- 6 oz of sliced deli roast beef
- 4 slices of tomatoes
- 2 thin slices of red onion, rings separated

Spread Mayonnaise on bottom layer of bread. Top with lettuce, roast beef and onion. Place other slice of bread and enjoy.

Antipasto Salsa and Chicken Wrap

Fresh, large tortillas are best for this. Find the nearest tortillaria and buy them there.

- 2 fresh tomatoes, skins removed, chopped
- ½ red onion, minced finely
- 1 Italian squash, diced
- ½ can artichoke hearts (packed in water NOT oil), chopped
- ½ cup roasted red peppers (jar variety okay)
- ½ cup fresh basil, chopped
- ¼ cup kalamata olives, coarsely chopped
- 1-2 tbs balsamic vinegar
- 1 tbs olive oil
- salt and pepper to taste
- 2 cups cooked chicken
- 8 flour tortillas

Mix all ingredients (except chicken) together in bowl. Chill for at least one hour. Fill tortillas with chicken and salsa. Serve.

Monte Cristo Sandwiches

Another classic – so easy and so good! Teach your kids how to make them so they can serve you breakfast in bed.

- 12 slices white bread
- 4 slices lean ham
- 4 slices cooked turkey
- 8 thin slices Swiss cheese
- butter
- 3 eggs beaten
- 1 tsp sugar
- 3 tbs milk
- salt and pepper
- powdered sugar
- strawberry jam

Butter four slices of bread and cover each with 1 slice each of ham and turkey. Butter the next 4 slices on both sides and place them on top. Cover each with 2 slices Swiss cheese. Butter the remaining slices and place on top. Trim crusts and cut each in half. Securing with toothpicks, dip in egg beaten with sugar and milk and salt and pepper to taste. Sauté in butter on both sides until golden brown. Remove picks, spread jam on top and dust lightly with powdered sugar.

Stuffed French Bread

All you need is a jug of wine and thou.

- 1 loaf French bread
- 8 oz cream cheese, softened
- 1 red pepper, roasted and sliced
- 1 jar artichoke hearts, drained of packing oil
- 1 tomato, diced
- 2 -4 oz of sliced pepperoni
- salt and pepper to taste

Slice bread lengthwise (bottom part should be thickest). Scoop out the middle to make room for stuffing, set aside. Process the cream cheese, red pepper, artichoke hearts, and tomatoes until smooth. Spread into bread. Season with salt and pepper to taste. Top with a layer of pepperoni. Cover then wrap in foil and chill for at least one hour before consuming.

Tapenade Cream Cheese Sandwich

- ½ cup Tapenade (store bought or home made - see appetizers)
- 6 eggs
- 4 oz cream cheese, cubed
- 2 tomatoes, sliced
- lettuce leaves
- 8 slices of whole grain bread

Beat eggs in a bowl, add cream cheese. Cook over medium heat in non-stick skillet. Toast bread and spread 4 bottom slices of bread with equal mixtures of Tapenade, followed by egg mixture. Top with tomato and lettuce and remaining bread slices.

Muffuletta Sandwich (pronounced moo-foo-*let*ta)

Originated in New Orleans by Italian grocery store owners. You can still find them there or stay here and make it. It will satisfy the biggest appetite.

- 1 large French bread loaf, sliced lengthwise
- 6 slices Genoa or other salami
- 6 slices Provolone cheese
- olive pickle mixture (see below)

Layer salami and cheese, top with olive pickle and serve.

<u>Olive Pickle</u>

- 1 celery stalk, chopped
- 1 garlic clove, crushed
- 1 can sweet red peppers, chopped
- 2/3 cup "salad" green olives (they're packed slightly crushed)
- 2 tbs cocktail onions, chopped
- 2 tbs capers
- 3 tbs olive oil
- 3 tbs red wine vinegar

Mix all ingredients in bowl.

Pan Bagna (*pon BON-ya*)

One of the first "box lunch" items. Italian farmers were sent off in the mornings with these sandwiches. You can serve them hot too. You can also add cooked sausage – but if you do that, eat it right away.

- loaf of French bread
- 2 tbs olive oil
- 1 medium onion, sliced
- 2 cloves garlic, minced
- 1 cup fresh tomatoes, diced
- 12 - 15 black olives, semi chopped
- 1 tbs dried oregano
- 1 tbs sugar
- 1 tsp salt

Sauté garlic and onions in oil over medium heat until onions are limp. Add tomatoes, black olives, oregano, sugar, and salt. Stir just enough to warm through then remove from heat. Slice one third top off loaf. Use hands to scoop out bread from bottom section of loaf. Fill with mixture. Replace top. To serve cold, wrap loaf tightly in foil, then place in plastic bag, Weigh down using a plate and cans. Refrigerate for 3 - 4 hours. Slice into sections to serve.

Barbecue Chicken Quesadilla

- 4 - 6 oz. cooked chicken
- barbecue sauce
- 1 tbs fresh cilantro, chopped
- ½ cup jack cheese (or Mexican style Quesadilla cheese), grated
- 4 flour tortillas

Scatter cooked chicken over a flour tortilla. Cover with cheese. Drizzle barbecue sauce over top, and then top with chopped cilantro. Cover with another tortilla. Repeat for second quesadilla. Place in microwave on medium high heat for about one minute (or until cheese melts).

Colorful Shrimp Quesadillas with Mango Salsa

- 2 tbs butter or margarine
- 1 cup onion, chopped
- kernels from 2 ears of fresh corn
- 1 garlic clove, minced
- 1 tomato, chopped
- 1 seeded jalapeño pepper, minced
- ¾ lb. medium shrimp, peeled, and chopped
- juice of two lemons
- 2 tbs fresh cilantro, chopped
- dash salt
- 8 flour tortillas
- 4 oz. mozzarella cheese, grated

Melt butter in large skillet over medium heat. Add onion, corn, and garlic. Sauté 30 seconds. Add tomato and jalapeño, sauté 4 minutes. Stir in shrimp, lemon juice, cilantro, and salt. Sauté 3 minutes or until done.

In separate dry skillet, heat flour tortilla over medium heat. Top with some cheese, then shrimp mixture. Top with more cheese, then top with another tortilla. Cook about 3 minutes until cheese is melted and tortilla is browned. Top with mango salsa (below)

Mango Salsa

- 2 tbs fresh lime juice
- 1/4 tsp salt
- 1/4 tsp fresh ground pepper
- 1/4 tsp fresh peeled ginger root, grated
- 1 cup fresh mango, diced
- 1 tomato, diced
- ¼ cup fresh cilantro, chopped
- 2 tbs green onion, chopped
- 1 - 2 tbs jalapeño pepper, minced and diced

Combine first four ingredients in small bowl. Add mango and remaining ingredients and toss gently.

Stuffed Portobello Mushrooms

Marinated Mushrooms

- ½ cup fresh cilantro, chopped
- ¼ cup fresh lime juice
- 1 tbs olive oil
- 2 tsp dried oregano
- 1 tsp ground black pepper
- 4 garlic cloves, minced
- 4 large Portobello mushrooms, gills and stems removed

Combine first six ingredients in zip locking plastic bag. Add mushrooms and chill for 15 - 20 minutes.

Stuffing

- 1 tsp olive oil
- ½ cup diced red pepper
- ½ cup diced yellow pepper
- ½ cup diced onion
- 4 cups good, dense bread, cubed
- ½ cup Monterey Jack cheese, grated
- ½ cup fresh parsley, minced
- 2 tbs water
- 2 large eggs, lightly beaten
- 2 tbs grated Parmesan cheese

Preheat oven to 350 degrees. Prepare stuffing by heating oil in large skillet over medium high heat. Add bell peppers and onions. Sauté about three minutes. Combine bell pepper mixture with bread crumbs in a separate bowl. Add cheese, parsley, water and eggs. Drain mushrooms and discard marinade. Place mushrooms on baking sheet and spoon stuffing onto mushrooms. Sprinkle with Parmesan cheese. Bake for 25 minutes or until stuffing is brown

Shrimp and Mango Tostadas

- 1 firm ripe mango, cubed
- 1 firm ripe avocado, cubed
- 6 tbs lime juice
- ¾ lb. shelled, cooked shrimp
- 1 tsp jalapeño or Serrano chili, seeded, and minced
- 1/3 cup green onions, chopped
- 4 flour tortillas
- 1 (16 oz.) can refried black beans
- ¼ cup chicken broth
- 3 cups iceberg lettuce, shredded fine
- ½ cup sour cream

Preheat oven to 400 degrees. Place mango and avocado in bowl. Add lime, shrimp, chili, and green onions, mix gently. Place tortillas on baking sheet and bake until lightly browned on one side. Turn over and brown. Combine beans and chicken broth in separate small bowl, microwave until soft. Place tortilla on plate. Spread bean mixture, then sour cream, then lettuce. Top with shrimp/mango mixture. Add salt to taste.

Dave Hinman helps Jeff prepare Bananas Foster during KVCR pledge special in 2002.

Steve Hammersmith prepares ostrich burgers during another pledge special.

Jeff interviews Shannon Woods and two "wenches" at a brew competition held at the Renaissance Faire in 1997. Also pictured are Greg Wyatt and Ed Beach.

Don Galleano at his winery in Mira Loma explains how grapes are grown in the Cucamonga Valley.

Jeff works on his kitchen set.

Appetizers

Red Wings

Inspired by two similar recipes from two different friends. One from Andre Allen, the other from Myron Mabre. Andre used drumsticks which he deep fried and coated with a hot sauce. Myron used wings (not deep fried) with a killer sweet-hot red sauce. I used Andre's deep fry process on wings then coated with Myron's sauce.

- 18 - 20 chicken wings
- 4 eggs - slightly beaten
- 1 cup flour
- vegetable oil for frying
- ¼ lb. butter
- 2 tbs brown sugar
- 2 -3 tbs Red Rooster brand Louisiana hot sauce

Chop tips off wings and discard, and then chop in half at joint to make "drumettes". Coat in egg, then dredge in flour. Place in frying pan with about 1 inch of oil heated over medium heat. Fry for about 8 minutes per side (or until inside is opaque and juices run freely). Place on paper towels to drain excess fat.

Melt butter in another skillet over low heat, add brown sugar and stir until melted. Stir in Red Rooster then remove from heat. Toss wings in this mixture to coat. Serve immediately.

Beer Boiled Shrimp

- 1 - 2 lbs medium shrimp, peeled, leave tail on
- 12 - 16 oz. Beer

Fill large pot half full of water, add beer. Bring to boil. Add shrimp, when most turn red, remove from heat (about 3 minutes, cut one in half, if solid white inside, it's done). Drain in colander. Serve with hot shrimp sauce (recipe below).

Hot Shrimp Sauce

- ¾ cup ketchup
- 1 tsp ground black pepper
- 1 tsp horseradish
- 1 tbs sugar
- Juice of one lemon
- ½ tsp Tabasco sauce (or any red pepper sauce)

Mix all ingredients, chill if you have time. Serve with shrimp.

Grilled Jalapeños stuffed with Sausage and Cheese

Thanks to Rob Weaver for this recipe. Ideally, cook them using a covered, kettle-type barbecue grill. Beware – these are very addicting. Don't make them alone or you're likely to eat them all in one setting.

- 24 large fresh Jalapeno chili peppers
- 8 oz uncooked ground pork sausage
- 8 oz sharp cheddar cheese, shredded
- 1 lb. bacon

Cut the tops off Jalapenos. Use a potato peeler to core out seeds and veins. Stuff each jalapeno with mixture of uncooked sausage and cheese. Wrap lengthwise with half strip of uncooked bacon. Secure with toothpick. Barbecue with grill cover on, medium, indirect heat for about 45 minutes. When bacon is crispy they are done.

Wally's Stuffed Jalapenos

This recipe is from my neighbor Wally Bain. I first tried these at one of the famous super bowl parties he and Debbie held. I can't remember much about the game that year, but I sure remember these tasty jalapeños!

- 24 Jalapenos- halved lengthwise and deveined (use fresh or marinated your choice)
- 6.5 oz can tuna in water, drained
- 4 oz can water chestnuts, chopped finely
- 2 tbs mayonnaise
- 4 oz cheddar cheese, finely grated

In a bowl mix tuna, water chestnuts, with enough mayonnaise to moisten. Stuff Jalapeño halves with mixture. Top with cheddar.

Mini Bean Tacos

- bag of round corn tortilla chips
- 1 can refried beans
- 8 oz cheddar cheese, grated
- 1 tomato, diced
- olives, sliced
- jalapeño, died
- green onions, diced

Spoon a little refried beans on each tortilla chip and place evenly on a large baking sheet. Place under broiler until chips begin to smell good. Remove. Top each chip with grated cheese, tomato, and remaining ingredients. Return to broiler and heat until cheese melts. Remove and serve immediately. Good with sour cream, salsa and guacamole.

Dr. C's Olive and Eggplant Tapenade

Dr. Costamagna (Doctor "C" for short) explained that Tapenade is a
French spread that begins with olives and capers. With a few Dr.
C "adds"
we render a fine spread that complements French bread, or crackers.
Enjoy with wine, or Dr. C's suggestion - beer.

- 1 6 oz can black olives
- 1 small eggplant - peeled, roasted, seeded and cut into quarters
  (ready for the food processor).
- 1 fresh garlic clove
- juice of one lemon
- 1 tbs capers
- 2 tbs Dijon mustard
- 1/4 cup olive oil (less if you wish)
- 2 tbs port sherry

Process all ingredients in food processor until consistency that will spread.

Fluffy Hummus Dip

My version of this great dip does not required olive oil, so it's lighter and sort of fluffy. My friends and family love it.

- 2 cloves garlic
- 12 oz garbanzo beans, drained
- ¼ cup Tahini
- 1 tbs dried cumin
- juice of two lemons
- 2 - 3 tbs water
- 2 tbs green onions, chopped
- salt and pepper to taste

Chop garlic in food processor. Add beans, Tahini, cumin, lemon juice, and water, puree until paste like (add more water if needed). Add salt and pepper to taste. Stir in green onions. Serve with pita bread, vegetables, bread, etc.

Eggs Remoulade (pronounced *rem*-oh-lawd)

- 2 tbs Creole mustard, brown mustard, or deli mustard
- 2 tsp paprika
- 1 tsp Louisiana pepper sauce (like Tabasco)
- 3 tbs tarragon vinegar
- ¾ cup olive oil
- 3 green onions, chopped
- 1 celery stalk, sliced
- 2 tbs fresh parsley, chopped
- salt and pepper to taste
- 6 hard boiled eggs peeled and halved.

Mix together mustard, paprika and pepper sauce. Add vinegar and stir.
Slowly whisk in olive oil until sauce is smooth. Correct with salt and
pepper. Stir in onions, celery and parsley. Chill for at least one hour. Serve
over eggs. Also good on cold meats and seafood.

Crab Cakes with Cajun Mayo

*The secret is frying the cakes in clarified (drawn) butter. Why clarify?
Butter tends to burn easily. But when you clarify, it renders the clear
looking part of the butter, which tends not to burn.*

- 10 - 12 slices fresh bread, crust removed, processed or torn up in small pieces
- 2 cloves fresh garlic
- 2 shallots (buy in veggie section - come in a small bag - near the onions)
- 1 green bell pepper, cored and seeded
- 1 red bell pepper, cored and seeded
- 1 lb cooked crab meat
- 1 tbs capers
- 4 tbs Dijon mustard
- 2-5 shakes Tabasco sauce
- 1 tsp dried pepper flakes
- 1 -2 eggs
- 1 stick butter, clarified (see instructions below)

Prepare fresh bread crumbs, set aside. Use food processor (or chop by hand)
and process garlic, shallots, green bell pepper, and red bell pepper together
until salsa like. Then mix in large bowl with crab, capers and mustard,
tobacco, and pepper flakes. Beat the two eggs then add. Make pancake
sized cakes and fry on medium low heat for 6 - 8 minutes per side in
clarified butter. Serve with Cajun Mayo.

Cajun Mayo:

Mix together (keep in fridge 'till ready to use)

- 1 cup mayonnaise
- 1 tsp paprika
- 1 tsp dry Cajun seasoning

How to clarify butter:

Place a stick of butter in a glass cup place in microwave oven, heat on high
for one minute. Skim off the top layer; pour the clear looking part into the
skillet. Leave the very bottom in the cup (and discard).

Classic Crab Cocktail

- 4 oz. crabmeat (fresh is best, fresh frozen better, canned acceptable)
- cocktail sauce (below)

Place crabmeat in chilled parfait dish or pilsner glass. Pour cocktail sauce over top.

Cocktail sauce:

- 2 tbs ketchup
- 1 tsp fresh lemon
- ½ tsp horseradish
- few drops Worcestershire sauce
- fresh ground pepper to taste

Mix ingredients in a small bowl. Chill until ready to use.

Corny Crab Cakes

- 6 slices of white bread
- ½ cup fresh parsley
- 1 bell pepper, seeded and quartered
- ¼ cup mayonnaise
- 1 large egg
- few drops hot pepper sauce
- ½ tsp ground cumin
- 1 6 oz can crab meat
- ½ cup canned corn
- olive oil for frying

Remoulade (see recipe below)

In a food processor, pulse bread until crumbs. Transfer to bowl. Add parsley to processor and pulse until fine. Add pepper and pulse until finely chopped. Add to bowl with bread crumbs. To bread crumb mixture add remaining ingredients. Form into small patties.

In a heavy skillet, heat oil over medium heat. Fry cakes on both sides until brown. Serve topped with Remoulade sauce (recipe follows).

Remoulade sauce

- 1 cup mayonnaise
- 4 tbs green onion, chopped
- ¼ tsp cayenne pepper
- ½ tsp ground cumin
- 2 tsp lime juice
- 1 tsp Dijon mustard

Combine and chill for at least one hour.

Crab Packages with Hoisan-Wine Sauce

Filling:
- 1 egg white, lightly beaten
- 12 oz crab meat (fresh best, but canned ok)
- ¼ cup green onions, minced
- 2 tsp fresh ginger root, minced
- 2 tsp fresh garlic, minced
- 1 tsp Chinese black bean paste
- 1 10 oz package frozen chopped spinach, thawed and drained

In medium bowl, beat egg white, and then add remaining ingredients. Mix well and set aside.

Hoisan-Wine Sauce:
- ½ cup Chinese Hoisan sauce (also called Chinese Barbeque sauce)
- 2 tbs white wine
- dash pepper

Mix all ingredients together, set aside.

Packages:

- juice of one orange combined with ½ cup water
- vegetable oil
- 1 package of egg roll wrappers (typically 30)
- 2 tbs corn starch or flour mixed with 4 tbs. water

Combine cornstarch and water. Set aside. Lay out one wrapper on dry surface. Place approximately one tablespoon of the crab mixture near the middle. Rub some of the cornstarch mixture on the bottom and right edges of the wrapper. Fold the other two (dry) edges down to make a triangle, seal with fingers. Fold remaining corners to form an "envelope". Set aside on platter lined with damp paper towels. Repeat.

In large skillet over medium high heat, add vegetable oil. Place 6 – 8 packages, smooth side down, in skillet . Add some orange/water to make steam, cover with lid and cook 2 minutes. Remove lid, turn packages over and continue cooking for 1 minute uncovered. Repeat process for remaining packages. Serve topped with Hoisan-Wine sauce.

Puffy Cheese Rolls

- 1 sheet frozen puff pastry, thawed per package directions
- parchment paper
- 3 tbs ricotta cheese
- 3 tbs sun dried tomatoes packed in oil, finely chopped
- 1 tbs grated parmesan cheese
- flour

Preheat oven to 350 degrees and line baking sheet with parchment paper. In small bowl, mix ricotta, tomatoes, and parmesan. Set aside. Spread out pastry on lightly floured surface. Roll out slightly more to 12" x 15" rectangle. Cover with thin layer of cheese mixture. Roll sides of pastry to middle. Cut into one inch slices. Place cut side up on parchment paper lined sheet. Bake for 15 - 16 minutes, or until golden brown and "puffy".

Garlic Lover's Shrimp

Fresh garlic and shrimp is a match made in heaven. The clam juice is the perfect compliment to the wonderful flavor of this dish.

- 12 cloves garlic, sliced
- ¼ cup olive oil
- 2 lbs medium to large shrimp, peeled and cleaned
- 1 fresh green chili, seeded and sliced thin
- 1 cup clam juice
- juice of 3 limes
- 2 tsp fresh parsley, chopped
- salt and pepper to taste

Heat olive oil in large skillet over low heat. Add garlic and gently stir for three minutes (don't let garlic get too brown). Remove garlic with slotted spoon (leaving oil in pan), place garlic on paper towel and set aside. Increase heat to medium. Add shrimp and chili to pan and stir until shrimp are done (turn pink and opaque through middle). Add clam juice and lime juice to pan and stir. Taste with salt and pepper, serve topped with fresh parsley.

Spicy Shrimp with Creamy Horseradish Dip

A perfect balance of hot and cool. The original recipe grills the shrimp.
You can also pan fry the shrimp in olive oil over medium high heat - like we
did on the show.

- 1 lb. large shrimp (12 - 16 count), peeled, cleaned, and patted dry
- wood or stainless steel skewers

Marinade:
- ¼ cup Chinese chili sauce or paste
- ¼ cup chili powder
- 2 tbs sugar
- 3 garlic cloves, minced
- 1 tbs ground cumin
- 1 tbs ground coriander
- 1 tbs red pepper sauce (like Tabasco)
- salt and pepper to taste

Dipping sauce:
- 8 oz heavy cream
- 1 - 2 tbs jalapeño pepper sauce (Tabasco makes one)
- 1 tbs prepared horseradish
- ¼ cup fresh cilantro, chopped

Prepare marinade by combining ingredients in medium bowl. Add shrimp
and marinade overnight in refrigerator. Prepare dipping sauce and chill.
Skewer shrimp and grill over hot coals until done (3 - 5 minutes per side).
Serve with dipping sauce.

Greek Style Sautéed Oysters

Serve these oysters with a chilled Retsina, an excellent wine that gets its unique flavor from fermentation in pine barrels. Find Retsina in Greek or Armenian markets.

- 1 cup dried (plain) bread crumbs
- 1 tbs fresh parsley, chopped
- 1 tsp dried oregano
- 1 tsp dried sage
- 1 tsp garlic powder
- ½ tsp ground black pepper
- 1/2 tsp salt
- 2 eggs slightly beaten
- 6 - 8 small oysters (or cut each medium sized oyster in half)
- 2 tbs butter
- 2 tbs olive oil

Mix bread crumbs with herbs in bowl. Dip oysters in egg, then coat with crumb mixture. Heat olive oil in frying pan over medium heat and then add butter. As soon as butter melts add the coated oysters. Sauté for 2 - 3 minutes per side, or just until firm and opaque (don't overcook). Serve with rice pilaf and salad with vinaigrette dressing.

Hot Artichoke Spread

My sister Barb used to bring these appetizers to parties, it was always a hit. Serve with big, thick wheat crackers.

- 1 cup Miracle Whip
- 1 cup grated Parmesan cheese
- 1 14 oz can artichoke hearts, drained and chopped
- 1 4 oz. can chopped green chilies, drained
- 1 garlic clove, minced
- 2 tbs green onions, sliced
- 2 tbs fresh tomatoes chopped

Mix first 5 ingredients and spoon into oven proof dish. Bake at 350 degrees for 20 - 25 minutes. Top with green onions and tomatoes. Serve with French bread or crackers.

Brandied Blue Cheese, Walnut and Pear Toast

An explosion of flavor – so robust, it's excellent served with a dry red wine.

- 4oz blue cheese, crumbles
- 2 tbs unsalted butter
- ¼ cup walnuts
- 1 French baguette, cut into1/4 inch slices
- 1 medium ripe pear, cored and thinly sliced

Let blue cheese and butter sit at room temperature for at least 30 minutes. Mash together with a fork until well combined. Stir in brandy and nuts. Layer bread on baking sheet and toast under broiler, until brown. Top each with one thin pear slice and some blue cheese mixture. Return to broiler and heat until cheese bubbles and serve

Pepperoni Lover's Cheese Ball

- 2 - 8 oz packages cream cheese, softened
- 4 oz pepperoni, minced
- 2 tbs green onions, chopped fine
- 4 oz. pine nuts, chopped fine
- milk

Mix the cream cheese, pepperoni, and green onions together, use a little milk to help mix. Form into ball. Roll in pine nuts to cover. Serve with crackers.

Pizza Spread

Make a batch of this before house guests arrive. It will be handy when you need a satisfying quick snack.

- 1 8 oz can tomato sauce
- 1 onion, chopped
- ½ tsp salt
- 3 squirts of garlic oil (or 3 cloves crushed fresh garlic)
- 1 lb of sharp cheddar cheese, grated
- ½ cup vegetable oil
- ½ tsp dried oregano
- 1 14oz can chopped olives
- parmesan cheese

Mix together and spread on buttered toast or bagel. Broil until hot then top with parmesan cheese.

The finished kitchen set is installed in the studio in 1997.
Jeff is pictured with Rusty Townshend (left), who designed and built the set,
and his assistant Randy Kristoffersen (right).

Preston Hayslette, studio manager
in 1997, adjusts Jeff's microphone
before a shoot.

Shari Underwood doing what she does
best, preparing ingredients for the shoot.

*Dan Underwood lending a hand behind the
camera before appearing on camera to
prepare a dessert.*

Camping show that was shot in our backyard.

Soups and Salads

Spinach Salad with Raspberries

- ½ cup plain nonfat yogurt
- ½ cup fresh of frozen raspberries, thawed
- 1 tbs skim milk
- 1 ½ tsp fresh mint, chopped
- 4 cups of fresh spinach
- ½ cup fresh mushrooms
- 1 tbs sesame seeds toasted
- 6 red onion rings
- 6 slices bacon, cooked crisp and crumbled

Combine yogurt, ¼ cup raspberries, milk and mint in small bowl, set aside.
In a large serving bowl place spinach, mushrooms and red onions in it.
Drizzle sauce then garnish with bacon, sesame seeds and raspberries and
mint.

Strawberry Spinach Salad

Everybody loved our shows featuring firefighters in the kitchen. Paramedic Jeff Heringer prepared this salad once. The strawberries and dressing are very tasty. You could almost serve this for dessert!

- 1 basket fresh strawberries, diced
- 2 bunches of spinach, cleaned and shredded for salad
- juice of 1 lemon
- 1 egg yolk
- ¼ cup powdered sugar
- 10 tbs vegetable oil

Wisk together lemon juice, egg yolk, sugar, and oil. Chill mixture for one hour. Toss with spinach and strawberries and serve.

Spinach Salad with Bacon and Creamy Dreamy Dressing

My mother in law, Shari always comes up with great recipes like this one. Make several copies of this recipe. Once your friends and family try it, they will want it.

Dressing
- ½ cup mayonnaise
- 2 tbs cider vinegar
- 2 tbs soy sauce
- 1 clove fresh garlic, mashed

Mix together and chill for at least one hour

Salad
- 1 bunch fresh spinach leaves, cleaned
- 1 lb. bacon, cooked, drained and crumbled
- 1 cup bean sprouts

Mix with dressing just before serving.

Spinach Gorgonzola Salad

Use a small, dry skillet to toast nuts or spices. It really brings out the flavor. It's one of those tricks that will make you a superior cook!

- 8 – 10 oz baby spinach, cleaned, dried
- 4 oz walnuts, crushed
- 4 oz. Gorgonzola cheese (or blue cheese)
- 1 red onion, peeled and sliced
- 4 oz. canned red bell peppers, sliced
- 2 hard boiled eggs, quartered

In small pan over medium heat, toast walnuts until fragrant. Remove from pan and set aside. In large salad bowl, mix spinach, walnuts, cheese, onion, and peppers. Toss with dressing. Top with eggs.

Dressing:
- 1 garlic clove, crushed
- ¼ cup tarragon vinegar
- 1 tbs fresh tarragon, chopped
- ½ cup olive oil

Crispy Spinach Salad

- 6 slices bacon, cooked, drained and crumbled
- 8 – 10 oz. baby spinach, cleaned and dried
- 1 medium onion, finely chopped
- 4 oz. water chestnuts, sliced
- 8 oz. fresh bean sprouts
- 2 hard boiled eggs, sliced

In large salad bowl, mix all ingredients together and toss with dressing. Top with sliced eggs.

Dressing:

- 2 tbs Worchester sauce
- 2 tbs sugar
- 2 tbs red wine vinegar
- ¼ cup olive oil
- ¼ cup ketchup

Combine ingredients and chill for one hour.

Spinach Salad with Curried Fruit and Nuts

- 2 lbs. fresh spinach leaves, cleaned
- 2 tsp sesame seeds
- ½ cup raisins
- 2 cups fresh apples, chopped
- 2/3 cup dry roasted peanuts
- 1/3 cup green onions, chopped

In medium sized skillet over medium heat, toast sesame seeds until they begin to brown, remove from pan and let cool. Mix with remaining ingredients and toss with dressing. Serve.

Dressing
- 2/3 cup salad oil
- 1/3 cup red wine vinegar
- 1 tbs chutney
- 1 tsp curry powder
- 1 tsp salt
- 1 tsp dry mustard
- ¼ tsp Tabasco sauce

Mix together and let stand at room temperature for 2 hours.

Raspberries with Feta Walnut Salad

- 2 green onions, finely chopped
- 1 tbs Dijon mustard
- ¼ cup raspberry vinegar
- 2 tbs balsamic vinegar
- 2 tbs honey
- 2 tbs fresh orange juice
- 1 cup olive oil
- ½ cups walnuts
- 4 cups baby greens
- 2 oz feta cheese, crumbled
- 1 cup fresh raspberries

To make raspberry vinaigrette, in small mixing bowl combine green onions mustard and vinegars. Add honey and orange juice whisk to blend. Add olive oil and whisk until well blended. In a large salad bowl, toss greens with ½ of the vinaigrette.

Place green mixture on four salads, plated and top with feta, raspberries and walnuts and drizzle remaining vinaigrette on top.

Pear, Spiced Pecan, and Blue Cheese Salad

- 1 large pear, sliced
- ½ cup pecans
- 1 tbs brown sugar
- 1 tbs butter
- pinch nutmeg or cinnamon
- 1 - 2 oz blue cheese, crumbled
- salad greens of choice
- 2 tbs balsamic vinegar
- 3 tbs olive oil
- 1 tsp sugar

Melt butter in skillet over medium heat. Add brown sugar and spice. Stir until well coated. Clean greens and dry on paper towel. Arrange salad greens on plates. Add pear, then pecans, and then top with blue cheese. Combine vinegar, oil, and sugar. Pour over top. Serve.

Pear, Cranberry & Pecan Salad

- 1 large ripe pear, sliced in 12 pieces
- ¾ cup dried cranberries
- ½ cup spiced pecans or walnuts
- crumbled blue cheese
- lettuce
- Balsamic Vinaigrette (see below)

Arrange salad greens on individual plates. Arrange 3 slices of pear on each plate, fanning out for presentation. Sprinkle on dried cranberries and pecans. Top with blue cheese. Drizzle dressing over all.

Balsamic Vinaigrette:
Combine two tablespoons balsamic vinegar with three tablespoons olive oil. Add 1 teaspoon sugar, stir until blended.

Xoriatiki (Greek Village Salad)

Perfect for hot summer nights when fresh vegetables are abundant. Don't forget to visit your nearest farmers market for veggies.

- 4 ripe tomatoes
- 1 cucumber
- 1 onion
- 1 green pepper
- 1/3 lb feta cheese
- olives
- capers
- ½ cup olive oil
- oregano
- salt

Cut the vegetables in slices and mix in a salad bowl. Top with the olives, capers and oregano and cover with "crumbled" feta cheese. Pour olive oil evenly over salad.

Pizza Salad

Remarkably satisfying! Gather your hungry crowd before compiling. You'll want to serve this immediately to keep the lettuce crisp.

- 1 lb ground beef
- 14 oz pizza sauce
- 3 - 4 oz thinly sliced pepperoni, separated
- 1 head iceberg lettuce, chopped
- 1 cup fresh tomato, chopped
- 2 cups mozzarella cheese, shredded
- ½ cup black olives, sliced
- cheese croutons

In medium skillet, brown ground beef and drain. Add pizza sauce and half the pepperoni. Heat through. In large salad bowl, layer half of the lettuce, meat mixture, and cheese. Follow with the rest of the lettuce, then remaining meat and cheese. Top with tomatoes, olives, remaining pepperoni, and croutons. Serve immediately.

Jicama Kiwi Salad

- 6 green lettuce leaves
- 1 head romaine lettuce, cut into bite sized pieces
- ¼ cup celery, chopped
- 1/ lb Jicama, peeled and cubed
- 2 tbs green onions, diced
- 3 kiwi, peeled and sliced
- 2 oranges, peeled and sliced
- ½ red onion, sliced

<u>Dressing</u> - combine the following:

- 1 tbs lime juice
- 2 tbs orange juice
- ¼ cup walnut oil
- salt and pepper to taste

Prepare dressing and chill. Line salad bowl with green lettuce leaves. In another bowl combine celery, Jicama, and green onions. Place romaine in center of bowl, then top with Jicama mixture. Top with circle of kiwi, orange, and red onion. Pour dressing over top.

Fried Chicken Salad

Chicken
- 2 – 3 boneless, skinless chicken breasts, sliced lengthwise
- ½ cup buttermilk

Soak chicken in buttermilk, chill for 30 minutes

Dressing
- ¼ cup honey
- 2 tbs Dijon mustard
- 1-2 tbs apple cider vinegar

Mix honey and mustard in small bowl. Wisk in vinegar until desired consistency is obtained. Chill until ready to use

Salad
- head of romaine lettuce, cleaned and separated into whole leaves
- 15 oz can baby beets, drained and sliced
- 2 oz crumbled blue cheese

Place 2-3 leaves lettuce on individual plates. Cover with beets and blue cheese.

Coating/fry
- ½ cup flour
- ½ cup dry breadcrumbs
- 1 tsp garlic salt
- 1 tsp Italian seasonings
- ground pepper to taste
- ¼ cup olive oil

Mix dry ingredients in shallow bowl. Drain buttermilk from chicken and then dredge chicken in mixture. Heat large skillet to medium heat, add oil, when oil is hot, add chicken to skillet and cook 3 minutes on each side or until done. Add to salad, cover with dressing and serve

Scallops in Watercress Salad

Imagine all of your most interesting friends together at one party. That's what this recipe makes me think of. It's chocked full of interesting ingredients – and they all work together. The tart flavor of the watercress complements the subtle flavor of the scallops.

- olive oil
- ½ red onion, minced
- 1 jalapeno pepper, seeded and minced
- 1 lb scallops
- 3 fresh tomatoes, diced
- 1 avocado, peeled and diced
- 1 bunch fresh cilantro, chopped
- juice of one lime
- 1 bunch watercress, trimmed
- 2 fresh garlic cloves, minced
- salt and pepper to taste

Bring 2 tablespoons of olive oil to medium heat in large skillet. Add onion and jalapenos, and sauté until onions begin to soften. Add scallops and cook until done (2-3 minutes, longer for larger scallops). Stir in remaining ingredients.

Arrange watercress in 4 bowls, top with scallop mixture

Green Goddess Shrimp Salad

To me, Green Goddess salad dressing stirs images of bee-hive hairdos and the music of Brazil 66. This dressing, popular in the 1960's was replaced in the 70's with granola and bulgar wheat. We brought it back because it's an excellent compliment to shrimp. Serve well chilled.

- 4 oz cooked small shrimp
- salad greens
- Green goddess dressing (recipe below)

Toss all ingredients, serve.

Green Goddess Dressing

- 1 cup fresh parsley leaves
- 1 garlic clove
- 3 green onions
- 3 anchovy fillets
- 1 tbs lemon juice
- 1 tbs tarragon vinegar
- 1 cup mayonnaise
- ½ cup sour cream
- salt and pepper to taste

In a food processor, finely chop parsley, followed by garlic, then green onions, then anchovy fillets. When this mixture has been finely chopped, transfer to bowl. Stir in remaining ingredients. Add salt and pepper to taste. Chill for at least one hour

Strawberry Chicken Salad

- 2 - 3 chicken breasts, cooked, diced
- 1 pint fresh strawberries, halved
- ½ cup celery, sliced
- ½ red onion, chopped
- 2 tbs sesame seeds, toasted in dry skillet
- 1 tsp dried tarragon
- 1 tbs olive oil
- 1 tbs balsamic vinegar
- ½ tsp paprika
- salt and pepper to taste

Combine chicken, strawberries, celery, and red onion in bowl. In another bowl, combine remaining ingredients and pour over chicken mixture. Cover and chill for one hour.

Cabbage Ramen and Green Onion Salad

- 3 3 oz packages Ramen noodles, broken up in to bite size pieces.
- 1 seasoning pack (from inside a Ramen package)
- 1 tbs rice vinegar
- 2 tbs sesame oil (vegetable oil ok)
- 1 tsp sugar
- 1 tsp soy sauce
- head cabbage (preferably Napa), sliced thin
- carrot, grated
- bunch green onions, chopped halfway up green part
- small package slivered almonds, toasted lightly

In a small bowl, mix together the dressing: seasoning pack, rice vinegar, sesame oil, sugar, soy sauce and set aside. Combine Ramen noodles, cabbage, carrot, green onions and almonds in a large salad bowl. Pour dressing over top, mix well and chill for 1 - 2 hours.

Thai Shrimp with Mushrooms

Find canned coconut milk in the Asian section of your grocery store. Don't accidentally buy the heavy, sweet stuff intended for tropical drinks.

- 12 oz unsweetened coconut milk
- ¼ cup dry white wine
- 2 tbs cornstarch
- 2 tbs water
- salt to taste
- 2 lbs medium shrimp, shelled, washed and pat dried
- ½ lb button mushrooms, stems removed and halved
- 2 tbs peanut oil
- 2 tbs butter
- 2 tbs garlic, minced
- ½ cup fresh basil, chopped
- ½ cup green onions, chopped
- 2 tbs lime juice

Prepare sauce by combining coconut milk and wine. Chill until ready to use. Heat wok or large skillet over high heat. Add oil and butter. As butter just melts (and before it starts to burn) add garlic. Stir for a moment then add shrimp. Cook shrimp until pink (2-3 minutes). Add mushrooms, basil and green onions, stir for a moment then add milk mixture. Bring to low boil. In a small bowl mix 2 tablespoons cornstarch and water and add to skillet to thicken milk. Stir in lime juice. Serve over thin noodles or rice.

Thai Cabbage Salad

Blanch the broccoli by cooking it for 3 minutes in your microwave oven, then immediately submerge eit in a bowl of ice water – that will "shock" it, which stops it from cooking further.

Dressing:

- juice from 3 limes
- 1 tbs toasted sesame oil
- 2 tbs soy sauce
- 2 tbs sugar
- 2 tsp fresh ginger, grated
- 3 garlic cloves, pressed

Remaining:

- 2 cups broccoli florets, blanched, and coarsely chopped
- 1 medium cabbage, shredded
- ½ cup carrot, shredded
- 2 tbs green onions, chopped
- 1/3 cup fresh cilantro, chopped
- 1/2 cup peanuts, halved

Combine all sauce ingredients in large salad bowl. Add broccoli, cabbage, green onions, carrot, and cilantro. Mix well. Top with peanuts before serving.

Pineapple Chili Cheese Slaw

- 1 can pineapple chunks in juice (reserve juice)
- 6 cups green cabbage, shredded
- 1 cup red cabbage, shredded
- 1 15 oz can dark red kidney beans, drained
- 1 4 oz can diced green chills
- 1, 4 oz can sliced ripe olives
- 6 oz cheddar cheese, shredded

Cumin Dressing

- ½ cup reserved pineapple juice
- ½ cup white vinegar
- 1 tsp ground cumin
- ½ tsp salt
- 1 clove garlic, pressed

Mix first ingredients. Add dressing. Toss and serve.

Cole Slaw with Mustard Sauce

- 2 tbs butter
- 2 tbs flour
- 2 tbs sugar
- ½ tsp ground black pepper
- 2 tbs Dijon mustard
- 1 cup chicken broth
- 1/3 cup white wine vinegar
- 4 cups red cabbage, shredded
- 4 cups green cabbage, shredded
- ½ cup red onion, chopped

Melt butter in saucepan over medium heat. Stir in flour and cook 1 minute. Add sugar, pepper, mustard, and chicken broth. Boil until mixture is thick. Add vinegar. Pour hot over cabbage and onion in large bowl. Mix well and serve. Note: Can chill mustard sauce first if you want a cold slaw.

Painted Desert Coleslaw

- ½ green cabbage, shredded
- 1 cup red cabbage, shredded
- 2 large carrots, shredded
- ½ small Jicama, shredded
- ½ small red onion, finely chopped
- 1 ½ cups apple, finely diced

<u>Dressing</u>

- ½ cup mayonnaise
- 1/3 cup white vinegar
- 2 tbs sugar
- 2 tbs Dijon mustard
- 1½ tsp caraway seeds
- ¼ salt
- pinch of ground black pepper

In a large bowl, combine vegetables and apples, tossing until mixed well. In a small bowl combine all the ingredients for the dressing. Mix thoroughly. Add dressing to vegetable and toss well.

Rice Salad with Olives and Artichoke Hearts

Another easy, tasty side dish. Always a hit at potlucks.

- 1 box Rice-a-Roni (chicken flavored)
- 1 can large pitted black olives, drained
- 1 jar artichoke hearts, not drained

Prepare Rice-a-Roni per package instructions. Add olives and artichoke hearts, mix well. Chill before serving.

Black Bean Salad in Bell Pepper Cups

- 2 15oz cans black beans, drained, rinsed
- 1 11oz can corn kernels, drained
- 1 medium red bell pepper, chopped
- 1 bunch green onions, chopped
- ¼ cup red onion, chopped
- 3 cloves of garlic, minced
- 2 tsp fresh basil, chopped
- 1 ½ tsp salt
- 1 tsp sugar
- 1 tsp pepper
- 1/3 cup red wine vinegar
- ¼ cup light olive oil
- 5-6 red (or green) bell peppers

In a bowl, combine the black beans, corn, red pepper, green onions, red onions, garlic and basil. In a small bowl, combine the salt, sugar, pepper, wine vinegar and olive oil. Whisk until well mixed. Pour over the black bean mixture and toss. Spoon mixture into bell peppers.

Roasted Potato Salad

- 2 lbs small red potatoes, quartered or halved
- 1 tbs vegetable oil
- 1 tbs stone ground mustard
- 2 tsp coriander seeds, crushed
- 6 garlic cloves, halved
- ½ cup fresh parsley, chopped
- ½ cup plain yogurt
- 3-4 green onions, chopped and separated
- salt and pepper to taste

Preheat oven to 400 degrees. Combine potatoes, oil, mustard, coriander, and garlic. Place in shallow roasting pan, bake for 30 minutes (or until potatoes are tender at middle-check with skewer or fork). Cool.

Combine remaining ingredients including half of green onions. Toss with cooked potatoes. Garnish with remaining green onions.

Red Potato and Portobello Salad

- 5 cups cooked red potatoes, cubed (or "dice sized")
- ½ cup green onions, sliced
- ½ cup parsley, chopped
- 3 tbs lemon juice
- 2 tbs capers
- 2 tbs balsamic vinegar
- ½ tsp dried basil
- ½ tsp dried oregano
- ½ tsp dried tarragon
- ¼ tsp black pepper, ground
- 8 garlic cloves, minced
- 2 portobello mushroom caps, thinly sliced

Cut the potatoes into small chunks. It will maximize the flavor of the salad.
Combine all ingredients except potatoes and mushrooms in a large bowl.
Add potatoes and mushrooms and toss well.

Mashed Potato Salad

- 2½ lbs thin skinned potatoes (small red or Yukon)
- 1 tsp salt
- ½ tsp pepper
- 6 tbs cider vinegar
- ½ cup olive oil
- ½ cup green onions, chopped
- ¼ cup parsley, chopped
- 2 hard-boiled eggs, peeled and chopped

Boil potatoes until tender and drain. While warm, place in a large bowl with salt and pepper. Mash slightly. Add vinegar then olive oil gradually and continue to mash. Leave lumpy. Stir in green onions, parsley, and eggs. Serve warm.

White Gazpacho

- 2 medium cucumbers, peeled and coarsely chopped
- 1 clove garlic
- 3 cups chicken broth
- 2 cups sour cream
- 1 cup yogurt
- 3 tbs white vinegar
- 2 tsp salt
- 2 tsp pepper
- 4 medium tomatoes, peeled and chopped
- ½ cup scallions (include tops), chopped
- 2 cup fresh parsley
- ½ cup toasted almonds (or sunflower seeds)

Throw the cucumber and garlic into a food processor (or blender) with a little bit of the chicken broth, then puree. Add the rest of the broth and blend. In another bowl, mix the sour cream and yogurt, then thin with about a third of the cucumber mixture. Add the rest of the cucumber mixture. Season with vinegar, salt and pepper. Chill for 6 - 8 hours. Serve in bowls. Use the tomatoes, scallions, parsley, and almonds as condiments.

Tropical Gazpacho

- 3 cups tomato juice
- 3 cups unsweetened pineapple juice
- 1 cup crushed pineapple
- 1 cup mango, diced
- ½ cup red bell pepper, diced
- ½ cup green bell pepper, diced
- ½ cup yellow bell pepper, diced
- ¼ fresh lime juice
- 2 tbs cilantro
- 1 tsp pepper
- ¼ tsp hot pepper sauce

Combine all ingredients and mix well. Cover and chill for 4-6 hours. Serve in bowls. Drizzle with Mexican cream (find in dairy section near cheese).

Southwest Chicken Soup with Hominy and Tomatoes

My uncle Jack McCurry made this soup at a family gathering up in June Lake. Easy to make – and you might have all the ingredients on hand.

- 4 cups chicken broth
- 12 oz can hominy, drained
- 2 - 3 whole roasted green chilies (canned okay), seeded and diced
- ¾ cup fresh tomatoes, diced
- 1 tbs lemon juice
- 1 cup chicken, cooked and diced
- 2 tbs green onions, chopped
- 3 -4 corn tortillas, cut into quarters
- ½ cup vegetable oil

Heat broth in pot, add hominy and chilies and bring to boil. Simmer for 5 minutes. Mix together tomatoes and lemon juice in a small bowl and set aside. Fry tortilla quarters in oil and drain on paper towel. Take broth mixture off heat and add tomato mixture, onions, and chicken. Spoon into bowls and top with tortillas. Serve immediately.

Avgolemono Soup (Ave-gho-leh-MO-no)

A wonderful Greek soup made from lemons and egg. The recipe is simple, pronouncing it is the challenge.

- 2 cups milk
- 2 tbs cornstarch
- 6 egg yolks, beaten
- ½ cup long grain rice
- 2 qt basic chicken stock
- ½ stick butter
- 1 cup fresh lemon juice

Stir the milk and cornstarch together and beat in the egg yolks. Set aside. Bring the stock to boil in a 4 qt. soup pot and add the rice. Reduce heat, cover and cook 25 min. Remove the soup form heat, add milk and egg mixture, stirring carefully. Continue to cook until all thickens. Remove from the heat again; add butter, and lemon juice. You may add some grated lemon peel and chopped parsley as garnish.

Easy Cheesy French Onion Soup

Easier to make than the traditional recipe, and less messy. Broil the cheese separately, on the bread, then place on top of the soup.

- 4 - 14 oz cans low salt beef broth
- 2 packages dry onion soup mix
- 5 medium brown onions, sliced
- 1 loaf French bread baguette
- 10 slices of Provolone cheese

Place broth, soup mix and onions in crock pot. Simmer on high for 3-4 hours, until onions are soft. Taste soup, if it's too strong, add hot water. Slice bread crosswise into ½ inch slices. Place bread slices on a baking sheet. Top with cut-up cheese. Broil until cheese melts. Ladle soup into bowls and top with cheesy bread slices. For an extra flare, sprinkle Parmesan cheese on top.

Hot and Sour Soup

Not only an excellent Chinese culinary favorite, but soothing for the common cold. It just might cure what ails you.

- 4 medium-size dried mushrooms (shitake or other Asian mushroom)
- ¼ lb boneless lean pork, cut in matchstick pieces
- 1 tbs sherry
- 4 cups chicken broth
- ½ lb chicken breast, skinned, boned and cut in matchstick pieces
- ½ cup sliced bamboo shoots, cut in matchstick pieces
- ¼ pound tofu, drained and cut into cubes
- 2 tbs white wine vinegar
- 1 tbs soy sauce
- 2 tbs corn starch
- ¼ cup water
- ½ to ¾ tsp white pepper
- 1 tsp sesame oil
- 1 egg, lightly beaten
- 2 whole green onions, cut in 1-inch diagonal slices

Cover dried mushrooms with warm water in bowl, let stand for 30 minutes, then drain. Cut off and discard stems; squeeze mushrooms dry and thinly slice. Combine pork with sherry; let stand for 10 minuets

In a 2 quart pan, heat chicken broth to boiling. Add mushrooms, chicken, pork and bamboo shoots. Stir several times, then reduce heat; cover and simmer for 5 minutes. Add tofu, wine vinegar, and soy; heat, uncovered for 1 minute. Blend cornstarch and water. Add to soup and cook, stirring, until lightly thickened. Turn off heat. Add pepper and sesame oil. Stirring continuously, slowly pour egg into soup. Sprinkle with green onions and salt

Roasted Potato and Garlic Soup

- 6 medium russet potatoes
- 2 tbs olive oil
- ½ tsp pepper
- 6 cloves garlic, peeled
- 1 medium onion, chopped
- 3 cups chicken broth
- 1 cup water
- 1 cup milk
- salt
- 4 oz. Colby cheese, grated

Preheat oven to 425 degrees. Peel potatoes and cut into 1 inch pieces. Place in shallow roasting pan, drizzle with olive oil and sprinkle with pepper. Bake 25 minutes. Turn potatoes over and toss with garlic cloves. Bake 20 minutes more, until brown. Remove and set aside 1 cup of roasted potatoes.

Heat remaining oil in a sauce pan over medium high heat. Stir in onion and remaining potatoes. Cook for 5 minutes. Stir in broth and water. Let simmer 20 minutes. Puree in food processor. Return to pan and thin with milk. Add 1 cup reserved potatoes and heat through. Serve topped with grated cheese.

Tortilla Soup

- 1 tbs vegetable oil
- 12 (6 inch) corn tortillas, cut into 1 inch slices, separated
- 1 brown onion, diced
- 1 jalapeño chili, seeded and diced
- 5 garlic cloves, minced
- 1 tbs tomato paste
- 2 14 oz cans whole tomatoes, un-drained
- 3 10.5 oz cans chicken broth
- 1 tbs ground cumin
- 2 cups cooked chicken breast, shredded
- 1 cup avocado, diced
- 1 cup cheddar cheese, shredded
- fresh cilantro, chopped

Heat oil in large Dutch oven over medium heat. Add half of the tortilla strips and cook 2 minutes or until crisp. Add onion, jalapeño, and garlic; sauté 3 minutes. Add tomato paste, tomatoes, cumin, and broth; bring to boil. Reduce heat and simmer for about 40 minutes.

Puree soup in blender. Return to Dutch oven to keep warm. Arrange smaller tortilla strips in one layer on baking sheet. Bake at 400 degrees for 7 minutes or until crisp. Place some chicken in bottom of soup bowls. Cover with soup. Top with cheddar, avocado, cilantro, and tortilla strips.

Cheese Beer Soup

Okay, it might not be the healthiest dish, but it sure tastes good! One of my personal favorites for cold winter days.

- 6 tbs margarine
- 1 large onion
- 1 cup celery, diced
- 1 cup carrots, diced
- ½ cup flour
- ½ tsp dry mustard
- 1 quart chicken broth
- 1/3 cup parmesan cheese
- 2 cups cheddar cheese, shredded
- 1 cup beer

Sauté onion, celery and carrots in margarine till barely tender. Add flour and dry mustard and mix well. Add hot chicken broth and stir. Simmer for 30 minutes. Take off heat, add cheeses and stir until melted. Just before serving, add beer; heat through, but do not boil. Serve with popcorn.

Albondigas Stew

There are many varieties of this classic Mexican meatball stew. This one's a "best of" recipe we developed from trying several different recipes throughout California.

Meatballs
- 1 lb ground beef
- ½ cup breadcrumbs
- ½ onion, minced
- ½ tsp ground cumin
- ¼ cup salsa

Mix ingredients together. Shape into meatballs. Place in (unheated) large skillet, when all meatballs have been formed, add 2-3 tablespoons water, turn up heat to medium high, cover skillet, and let meatballs simmer until done.

Soup
- vegetable oil
- 1 medium onion, chopped
- 1 small can chopped green chilies
- 1 tbs fresh garlic, minced
- 16 oz. sodium-free chicken broth
- 14 oz. can sodium-free chopped tomatoes, un-drained
- ½ cup salsa

Heat in large pot or Dutch oven on medium heat. Cover bottom with veggie oil and heat. Add onions, chilies, and garlic. Stir until onions are soft. Add remaining ingredients, bring to boil. Reduce heat and simmer for 10 minutes. Add meatballs. Serve with garnishes – below.

Garnishes
- avocado, sliced
- fresh cilantro, chopped
- corn tortillas, sliced, placed on baking sheet and toasted in 425 degree oven until brown

107

Bourbon Corn Chowder

When the alcohol has dissipated, bourbon takes on a new flavor which complements food. This dish is fun because you get to flame the bourbon. Be careful!

- 4 tbs unsalted butter
- 1 small onion, diced
- 2, 14oz cans of creamed corn
- ¼ cup bourbon
- ¼ tsp. nutmeg
- 2 - 3 drops hot red pepper sauce
- ½ cup chicken broth
- ½ cup heavy cream
- salt and pepper to taste

Melt butter over medium heat in large heavy pan. Sauté onions until soft. Stir in creamed corn. Heat bourbon in separate small sauce pan, carefully ignite and add to corn. Stir in remaining ingredients and serve immediately.

Hearty Clam Chowder

- 1 cup water
- 3 cans clams, chopped (reserve juice)
- 2 cups potatoes, diced
- 2 cups carrots, sliced thin
- 2 medium onions, chopped
- 2 tbs parsley, chopped
- 2 chicken bullion cubes
- 1 can cream of celery soup
- 2 cups milk
- 8oz jack chasse, shredded
- salt and pepper to taste

In sauce pan put water and clam juice. Add carrots, potatoes, onions, and bullion cubes. Simmer until tender, and then add clams, parsley, soup and milk. Heat thoroughly. Serve with jack cheese.

Crab and Sweet Corn Bisque

You can whip this up in no time. A hearty and tasty indulgent treat. Enjoy on a cool fall day.

- 4 cups whole milk
- 2 – 3 raw potatoes, cubed (small red, or Yukon Gold)
- 1 lb medium to large shrimp, (peeled and cleaned)
- 1.5 tsp Creole seasoning
- ¼ tsp salt
- ¼ tsp pepper
- 2 14 oz cans cream corn

In medium to large saucepot bring milk to simmer. Stir in Creole seasoning, salt, and pepper. Add potatoes and simmer for 10 minutes. Add shrimp and cook 2 – 3 minutes, or until done. Stir in corn until warmed. Serve immediately.

Mushroom Sausage Soup

Count on everybody loving this hearty and satisfying soup. Spend an extra dollar and buy the premium, lean breakfast sausage.

- ½ lb bulk pork sausage
- 1 large onion, chopped
- 1 large carrot, thinly sliced
- 1/3 lb mushrooms, thinly sliced
- 5 cups beef stock or beef broth
- 1/3 cup pearl barley
- 1/2 tsp thyme

Heat a 3-quart pan over medium heat; when pan is hot, crumble sausage into it and cook, stirring occasionally, until lightly browned. Add onion, carrot, and mushrooms; cook, stirring, until onion is soft (about 10 minutes). Stir in stock, barley, and thyme. Bring to a boil over medium-high heat; reduce heat, cover and simmer until barley is tender (about 30 minutes). Skim and discard fat or let cool, then cover and refrigerate, removing solidified fat the next day. Reheat slowly until steaming.

Roasted Tomato and Pesto Bread Stew

- 4 cups chicken stock
- 6 large tomatoes, halved
- 2 cups fresh basil leaves
- 2 oz pine nuts or walnuts
- 2 tbs Parmesan cheese
- 1 loaf Italian bread
- olive oil
- salt
- fresh ground pepper

In oven, place top rack in upper third of the oven. Preheat oven to 400 degrees. Place tomato halves (skin side down) on large baking sheet. Drizzle with olive oil. Sprinkle with ample amounts of salt and pepper. Place on top rack in oven, roast for 30 – 40 minutes, or until fully cooked. Remove and cool.

Make pesto by placing basil leaves in blender or food processor, followed by pine nuts and olive oil, puree. Blend in Parmesan cheese and salt and pepper to taste. Set aside.

Bring chicken stock to boil in large sauce pan or Dutch oven. When tomatoes have cooled enough to handle, use a spoon to scoop tomato from skins and into broth. Discard skins.

Stir pesto to tomato / broth mixture, bring to boil. Tear bread into small pieces and add to broth. Stir well until bread has mostly dissolved into broth.

Classic Oyster Stew

Growing up, I looked forward to oyster stew every Christmas Eve at my grandmother's house, where our whole family would gather to enjoy great food she'd prepared. Later, she'd march us down to the church for candlelight services.

- 2 cups potatoes, peeled and diced
- ½ cup onion, peeled and diced
- ½ cup celery, diced
- 1 tsp minced garlic
- 2 bay leaves
- 2 tbs butter
- 1 cup water
- 1 cup clam juice
- strained liquid from the oysters plus enough water to make 2 cups
- ½ cup vermouth or dry white wine
- 1 cup half-and-half
- 1 tsp hot pepper sauce
- ½ tsp salt
- 2 pints small fresh oysters, drained , liquor reserved
- green onions, chopped

In a large soup pot over medium heat, add the potato, onion, leek, celery, garlic, bay leaves, butter, water and clam juice. Cover and gently simmer about 10 minutes. Add the second broth and wine; continue simmering another 15 minutes until the potatoes are soft. Remove the bay leaves. Add the half-and-half, hot pepper sauce and salt. In a separate medium saucepan, heat the oysters just until edges curl. Stir oysters plus any accumulated juices into stew. Sprinkle with scallions and serve.

113

The crew takes a break in 1998. Pictured left to right: Shari Underwood, Dan Underwood, Lee Underwood, and Ed Beach.

A cure for the summer time blues in 1998 - our "Kids in the Kitchen" show. Left to right: Alex Baker, Chris Baker, Andi Underwood (Dan's daughter), Jill Baker, and Jeff.

Side Dishes

French Bread with Green Onions and Cheddar

Indulge! It's another great one from the firefighters of Staion 66 in Chino Hills, California.

- 4 oz. cheddar cheese, shredded
- 2 tbs mayonnaise
- 2 tbs green onions, chopped
- 1 loaf French bread, sliced lengthwise into two sections
- 2 to 3 tbs butter or margarine

Preheat oven to 400 degrees. Mix together mayonnaise, cheddar, and green onions. Spread butter on bread, followed by cheddar mixture. Place on baking sheet in oven for 10 minutes or until cheese bubbles.

Jalapeno Cornbread

- 4 tbs oil
- 1 cup medium-grind cornmeal
- 1 cup flour
- 2 tbs sugar
- 1 tbs baking powder
- 1 tsp salt
- 1 cup buttermilk
- 1 cup corn kernels
- 1 cup cheddar cheese, grated
- 3 eggs, lightly beaten
- 3 jalapenos, minced
- 2 tbs minced onion
- 2 tbs sour cream
- ¼ cup unsalted butter, melted

Grease a 10-inch cast-iron skillet with 1 tablespoon of the oil. Place the empty skillet in a cool oven and set the oven at 400 degrees. In a medium bowl, stir together the cornmeal, flour, sugar, baking powder and salt. Pour in the buttermilk and add corn, cheese, eggs, jalapenos, onion and sour cream. Gently mix by hand. Stir in the melted butter and remaining oil. Remove the skillet from the oven, pour the batter into the skillet and return to oven. Bake for 30 minutes, or until it begins to brown.

117

Chili Corn Bread Bake

- 2 small boxes of corn bread mix (add eggs and milk)
- 1 14oz can corn, drained
- 1 14oz can stewed tomatoes, drained
- 2 14oz cans chili
- 1 lb. cheddar cheese, grated

Preheat oven to 350 degrees. Prepare both boxes of corn bread (together) per instructions on box. Mix in canned corn. Pour half of bread mixture into bottom of buttered lasagna pan. Layer chili, tomatoes and cheese. Top with remaining bread mixture. Bake for 45 min to one hour (until top layer of corn bread looks done).

Veggie Pancakes with Feta and Tomato

- 2 eggs
- ½ cup vanilla yogurt
- 1¼ cups biscuit baking mix
- 1 tbs vegetable oil
- 1 onion
- half of one green bell pepper, seeded
- half of one red bell pepper, seeded
- 1 tsp fresh parsley, chopped
- 4 oz feta cheese, crumbled
- 2 tomatoes, sliced

In a medium bowl blend eggs, yogurt and biscuit baking mix. Use a food processor to chop onion, green pepper, and red pepper. Heat oil over medium heat. Sauté onion, green bell pepper and red bell pepper, until tender; stir into batter.

Heat a lightly oiled griddle or frying pan over medium high heat. Pour or scoop the batter onto the griddle, using approximately 1/4 cup for each pancake. Brown on both sides and serve hot, garnished with feta, tomatoes, and parsley

Potato Cheese Pancakes

In addition to dinner, this is also a great brunch item. It's also perfect for late nights when you come home hungry.

- 12 oz frozen hash browns
- 1 cup mozzarella cheese, grated
- ½ cup sour cream
- 2 large eggs, slightly beaten
- ¼ cup milk
- 2 green onions, diced
- ½ tsp ground cumin
- ¼ cup flour
- salt and pepper to taste

Stir together all ingredients. Fry with some vegetable oil in cast iron pan over medium heat. About 3 - 4 minutes per side.

Oyster Stuffing

Thanksgiving and Christmas dinners were not complete without Oyster stuffing. This is an old family recipe. I hope you make it yours.

- ¼ cup celery, chopped
- ¼ cup onion, chopped
- ¼ cup carrot, grated
- 2 tbs butter
- ¼ cup butter, melted
- 1 box dressing mix
- 3 oz cashews
- 6 oz jar fresh small oysters (if medium, cut in half), liquor (juice) reserved
- 1 tbs lemon juice
- ¼ cup fresh parsley, chopped

Sauté celery and onion in 2 tablespoons butter until soft, stir in carrots. Pour into bowl. Add dressing mix, cashews, lemon juice, parsley, and oysters. Mix well. Add equal parts oyster liquor and melted butter until stuffing is no longer dry. Bake in casserole dish 30 - 40 minutes at 350 degrees.

Onion and Cheese Casserole

Grandma Bowman was famous for this recipe. It was featured as a side dish on our first Thanksgiving show. It's been one of our most requested recipes over the years. Try it and you'll see why.

- 8 whole, medium brown onions, skin removed
- 1 large bag potato chips
- 1 lb cheddar cheese, grated
- 1 can cream of mushroom soup
- 1 cup onion broth (saved from onion boil)

Boil whole onions in 12 - 16 quart pot until soft all the way through (45 min to one hour). Reserve one cup of onion broth, then drain onions and let cool. Smash potato chips in bag.

Butter lasagna pan, spread 1/3 of chips in bottom of pan. Layer half the onions next followed by half the cheese. Layer more chips, then rest of onions, topped by rest of cheese and finally a layer of chips. Mix mushroom soup with onion broth then pour over top. Bake 45 minutes on 350 degrees. Let cool 15 minutes before serving (to set up).

Better Than Ice Cream Baked Beans

Back when my wife Donna was my fiancé, she brought this dish to a family reunion picnic. My relatives praised the dish, stating that it tasted "better than ice cream". That name stuck.

- 1 64 oz can baked beans, undrained
- 1 32 oz can kidney beans, drained
- 1 32 oz can pinto beans, drained
- 1 lb bacon, cooked and crumbled
- 1 onion, chopped
- ½ cup ketchup
- ½ cup brown sugar
- 1 tsp Worchester sauce
- 1 lb cheddar cheese, cubed
- 1 cup (or more) grated parmesan cheese

Mix everything except the parmesan cheese together. Pour into a buttered casserole dish. Top with lots of parmesan cheese. Bake at 350 degrees for 45 minutes. Allow 20 minutes to cool and set up before serving.

Smashed Potatoes

- 4 red potatoes
- 4 Yukon potatoes
- 6 tbs cider vinegar
- ½ cup olive oil
- ½ cup green onion, chopped
- ¼ cup parsley, chopped
- 2 eggs, hard boiled, peeled and chopped
- salt and pepper to taste

Boil potatoes with skin on. Drain and let cool 10 minutes. Transfer to bowl, season with salt and pepper, then smash slightly. Add vinegar and olive oil gradually while smashing. Stir in green onion, parsley an eggs. Serve warm.

Chorizo Beans with Rum

Upon tasting this, you'll likely make it your favorite "baked bean" recipe.

- ½ package pork or beef chorizo (5 – 6 oz.)
- 1 onion, minced
- 5 fresh garlic cloves, minced
- 1 to 2 jalapeno peppers, seeded and minced
- ½ cup ketchup
- ½ cup molasses
- ½ cup rum
- ½ cup brown sugar
- 2 tbs Worcestershire sauce
- 1 15 oz can kidney beans, drained
- 1 15 oz can pinto beans, drained
- 1 15 oz. can black beans, drained
- Louisiana hot sauce for flavor

Bring large Dutch oven to medium heat and cook chorizo for at least 5 minutes, don't drain. Add onion, garlic, and jalapenos and cook until onions are soft. Stir in remaining ingredients (except beans), bring to boil, reduce heat and simmer for 5 minutes. Add beans and hot sauce. Simmer for one hour over low heat.

Spicy Spanish Rice

This dish uses store-bought Spanish rice mix and spices it up. <u>NOTE</u>: don't use the rice mix that requires canned tomatoes.(You likely know the one I mean)

- 2 boxes Spanish rice mix (calls for butter and water)
- 1/3 cup of white rice (extra)
- 1 tbs dried cumin powder
- ½ tbs dried garlic powder
- 2 cubes chicken bullion
- 1 14 oz can *Rotel* brand tomatoes, not drained
- 1 green bell pepper, chopped
- 1 bunch green onions, chopped halfway up
- 1 14 oz can Mexicorn, drained and heated separately

Use a large pot and prepare packages of rice per directions on box including water, butter, and spice packages. Add the remaining ingredients noted above except the Mexicorn. Cook covered for 25 minutes on low heat. Before serving, stir in the heated Mexicorn.

Balsamic Roasted Potatoes

- 8 red potatoes, quartered
- 2 tbs olive oil
- 2 tbs butter
- 2 -3 tbs balsamic vinegar
- 1 tsp rosemary
- 1 tsp parsley
- salt and pepper to taste

Heat oven to 425 degrees. Heat butter and olive oil in medium skillet. Add potatoes, rosemary, and parsley. Sauté 2 to 3 minutes. Mix in balsamic vinegar. Pour potatoes onto rimmed baking sheet. Place in over for 20 minutes. Remove and sprinkle with salt and pepper to taste.

Garlic Lover's Refried White Beans

Inviting vegetarians over for a dinner party? Make this dish for them. In fact, make a double batch, because the carnivores will love it too. And if you are lucky, you'll have leftovers - it's even better the next day.

- 3 tbs vegetable oil
- 1 carrot, grated or diced
- 1 bunch green onions, chopped (at least 1 cup)
- 6 large garlic cloves, minced
- 1 tbs dried cumin
- 1 14 oz cans great northern or other white beans, un-drained
- 1/3 cup fresh cilantro, chopped

Heat a large skillet to medium heat. Add carrots and sauté for 3 minutes. Add green onions and garlic. Sauté for another 3 minutes. Stir in cumin and beans. Partially mash with potato masher. Reduce heat and cook another 10 - 15 minutes. Finish mashing to desired texture.

Sweet Potatoes with Tequila and Lime

Looking for something different to bring to the family holiday dinner? Bring this one; it will stand out on the buffet table. And it's tasty!

- ½ cup butter
- 5 lbs sweet potatoes, peeled and grated
- ¼ cup sugar
- 1/3 cup tequila
- ¼ cup lime juice
- salt and pepper to taste
- lime wedges

Pre-heat oven to 475 degrees. Place butter in 2" x 12" x 14" baking pan. Put pan in oven to melt butter. Add grated sweet potatoes and sugar to pan and bake for 50 - 60 minutes turning occasionally (be careful not to mash). Add tequila and lime juice and bake for 5 minutes more. Pour into serving dish and garnish with lime wedges. Serve immediately.

Roasted Corn on the Cob

We featured this on a "camping" show, in which we prepared recipes perfect for the campground. We shot the whole show in our backyard – we set up a tent and everything. I was amazed at how many viewers thought we were actually in the woods! (I bought a lawn mower after that).

- 10 - 12 ears of corn on the cob, un-shucked
- ½ cup vegetable oil
- 2 tbs soy sauce
- bunch of aluminum foil

Mix the oil and soy sauce. Peel off one husk of the corn without removing. Brush the soy sauce mixture over the raw corn. Replace the husk. Repeat on other side. Wrap in foil. Repeat with rest of corn. Roast over medium hot coals for 45 minutes.

Corn with Chili and Cream Cheese

I liked this recipe because the cream cheese and green chili offers a tasty twist to yellow corn.

- 3 tbs unsalted butter
- 2 garlic cloves, minced
- 6 oz cream cheese, softened, cut in chunks
- ¼ cup milk
- 4 cups corn kernels
- ½ cup roasted green chili, chopped
- ½ tsp salt
- ½ tsp fresh ground black pepper
- ½ cup dry bread crumbs
- paprika

Preheat oven to 350 degrees. Butter a medium baking dish. Sauté garlic in butter until soft. Add cream cheese and milk. Reduce heat and cook until cheese melts. Remove from heat. Mix in corn and green chilies. Add salt and pepper to taste. Pour mixture in baking dish. Top with bread crumbs and paprika. Bake for 25 minutes or until bubbly.

Green Beans with Pecan Caramelized Onions

- 8 oz fresh green beans
- ice
- tbs fresh orange juice
- 1 tbs Dijon mustard
- 1 tbs light brown sugar
- 2 tbs unsalted butter
- 1 small red onion, thinly sliced
- 1/3 cup pecans, coarsely chopped
- 1 tsp fresh thyme, lightly chopped

Fill a medium sized bowl with ice water. Fill sauce pan with salted water and bring to boil. Get timer ready. Drop green beans in boiling water - set timer for 4 minutes. When time is up, remove beans (don't worry about boiling status). Drop beans in ice water for 3 minutes. Drain and dry.

In small bowl mix orange juice, mustard, and brown sugar. In large skillet, melt butter over medium low heat. Add red onion and pecans. Toss to coat. Increase heat to medium high and cook until onions are soft (8 - 10 minutes). Layer beans over onion mixture, followed by thyme and some salt and pepper. Add mustard mixture and toss in pan for 2 minutes or until thick. Serve immediately.

Green Beans and Tapenade

- 1 lb green beans, ends trimmed
- ¼ cup Tapenade (see recipe under appetizers)
- 1 clove garlic, minced
- 1 tbs olive oil
- olive tapenade (store bought or home made)

Steam green beans for 3 minutes . Transfer to bowl of ice water to stop cooking process ("shock"), drain. Transfer to serving bowl and toss with Tapenade, garlic, and olive oil.

Garlic Roasted Asparagus with Parmesan

- 10 – 12 spears fresh asparagus, cleaned and trimmed
- 2 –3 cloves fresh garlic, minced
- ¼ cup olive oil
- ½ cup fresh Parmesan cheese, grated
- Aluminum foil

Preheat oven to 425 degrees. Spread foil on cookie sheet. Place asparagus on sheet. Mix olive oil and garlic. Use pastry brush to spread oil mixture over asparagus. Sprinkle with cheese. Bake 10 – 15 minutes or until done.

Asparagus with Orange Butter Sauce

Each year the Orange Blossom Festival is held in Riverside. Occasionally they gave me the opportunity to participate in their "Celebrity Chef Theatre". All day chefs from the area prepare dishes featuring oranges in front of a live audience.

When it came my turn, I had trouble getting the water to boil to cook the asparagus. It was taking too long, and I was running out of banter to keep the crowd interested. Luckily, the chef before me had used a barbecue grill, and it was still hot. I simply transferred the asparagus to the grill and cooked it that way! Either cooking method results in a tasty way to enjoy asparagus..

- 1 lbs fresh asparagus
- ½ tsp salt
- 2 medium oranges (1 to render ¼ cup orange juice, other for garnish)
- 1/3 cup butter, clarified
- ground pepper to taste

Snap off ends of asparagus. Lie in medium skillet and cover with boiling water. Add salt and cook over medium heat for until done (5 - 10 minutes).

Peel first orange and slice thinly (for garnish). Grate second orange to get 2 tablespoons rind, then render juice. In small saucepan, combine clarified butter, orange juice, and rind. Reduce until thickened.

Cover cooked asparagus with sauce. Serve.

134

Steamed Eggplant with Chili Sauce

Use Chinese eggplant- it's smaller and thinner than typical eggplant. The steamer is easy to make (instructions below)

- 1.5 lbs Chinese eggplant
- 1 tbs oil
- 1 tbs fresh garlic, minced
- 1 tbs fresh ginger, minced

Sauce ingredients:
- 3 tbs soy sauce
- 2 tbs red wine vinegar
- 2 tbs sugar
- ¼ tsp salt
- 1 tbs toasted sesame oil
- 1 tsp chili paste with garlic

Quarter eggplant lengthwise and place on a plate. Steam until limp. Meanwhile, combine sauce ingredients in bowl and stir. Heat wok or skillet over medium heat. Add oil, then stir fry garlic and ginger just until aroma develops. Pour in sauce, bring to boil. Pour over steamed eggplant and serve.

Home made steamer:

Remove both ends of empty short can (tuna, water chesnuts, etc). Place in bottom of stock pot. Add enough water to cover top of can. Place plate of eggplant on can. Cover and bring to boil. Check for water level occasionally.

Balsamic Veggie Medley

- 2 tbs vegetable oil
- 2 tbs plus ¼ cup balsamic vinegar (separated)
- assortment of chopped vegetables (squash, red cabbage, peppers, asparagus, onion, zucchini, etc).
- 1 tbs sugar

Heat oil in large sauté pan or wok over medium high heat. Add chopped vegetables and stir fry for 2 - 3 minutes. Add ¼ cup vinegar and reduce heat to medium low, stirring occasionally. When vegetables appear done, add remaining vinegar and sugar, stir and serve.

Hot Spinach with Lemon and Currants

- 1 tbs butter
- ¼ cup dried currants
- ¼ cup mined lemon (including peel)
- 1 tsp sugar
- 1 lb fresh spinach leaves, rinsed and drained
- ½ tsp nutmeg, ground
- salt

In a medium saucepan over high heat (can be done in a wok) stir in butter, currants, lemon and sugar until lemon in slightly brown, about 3 minutes. Put mixture in a bowl.

Add spinach leaves and nutmeg to pan. Continually stir until spinach is wilted, about 2 – 3 minutes. Stir in currant mixture and salt and pepper to taste.

Hot Cabbage with Red Chili

- 2 fresh red chili peppers, seeded and sliced thin
- 2 tbs butter
- 1 head cabbage, sliced
- 1/3 cup water
- salt and pepper to taste
- 2 tsp cider vinegar
- 1 tsp ground cayenne pepper

Heat butter over medium heat in frying pan. Add butter and chili strips and cook until they begin to curl. Add cabbage and water. Cover and lower heat for 3-4 minutes. When cabbage has wilted, uncover and continue cooking until liquid has been reduced. Correct with salt and pepper. Stir in vinegar and cayenne just before serving.

Cabbage with Onion and Orange

- 1 head cabbage, sliced
- 1 medium onion, sliced
- 3 tbs butter
- ½ cup orange marmalade
- 3 tbs Balsamic vinegar

Put cabbage and onion in microwave-proof bowl, cover with plastic wrap - cook in Microwave for 10 - 12 minutes on high - stir halfway through cooking. Drain excess liquid.

Meanwhile melt butter in saucepan over medium heat. Add marmalade and vinegar. Mix with cabbage/onion and serve.

Red Cabbage with Wine

A perfect compliment to grilled steak

- ½ head of red cabbage, shredded
- 1 medium onion, thinly sliced
- 2 granny smith apples, cored and sliced
- 2 tbs butter
- ¼ cup red wine
- 1 tbs caraway seeds
- 1 tbs cornstarch, mixed with a little water.

Sauté the onions and apples in the butter until onions are soft. Cover and simmer for 40 minutes. If needed, thicken sauce with cornstarch mixture. Serve warm.

Coleslaw with Mustard Sauce

- 2 tbs butter
- 2 tbs flour
- 2 tbs sugar
- ½ tsp ground black pepper
- 2 tbs Dijon mustard
- 1 cup chicken broth
- 1/3 cup white wine vinegar
- 4 cups red cabbage, shredded
- 4 cups green cabbage, shredded
- ½ cup red onion, chopped

Melt butter in saucepan over medium heat. Stir in flour and cook 1 minute. Add sugar, pepper, mustard, and chicken broth. Boil until mixture is thick. Add vinegar. Pour hot over cabbage and onion in large bowl. Mix well and serve.

Mrs. Wyatt's Famous Sauerkraut

Greg Wyatt has always been instrumental to our show. A multi-talented cat who's always a pleasure to have around. His mother's recipe is excellent. Just be sure to follow it exactly!

- 1 large can sauerkraut
- 1 apple, cored and sliced
- 1 onion, sliced
- 1 tsp caraway seed
- ¼ cup catsup
- ¾ cup brown sugar

Mix all ingredients in heavy pot. Simmer (do not boil) for 2 hours.

Sampling food after a shoot. Pictured left to right: Alex Baker,
Dan, Jeff, Frank Salvo, Ed Beach

Jim Patrick (right) was the studio manager in 1999. Here,
he takes a break in the control room with Greg Wyatt.

These two doctors were regular guests on the show in the early days.
They prepared healthy meals such as ice cream pie and Oxtail stew.
Pictured left to right: Ed Beach, Maureen and Dr. Hector
Costamagna, Donna Baker, and Dr. Steve Pulverman.

Main Entrees

Margarita Chicken

In the early days, we shot the show in our kitchen. Just before shooting (and for no logical reason) we decided to change the name of this dish to "Margarita ville Chicken". While preparing the dish, I decided to ask the crew a few Jimmy Buffet trivia questions. I awarded the winners by throwing them stuff I found around the kitchen. Prizes included a broken potato peeler, a near-empty can of coffee, and a cilantro sprig. That was the show in which the crew turned on me at the end and pelted me with limes. (And some people say there's no quality television these days).

- 4 boneless, skinless, chicken breasts
- ½ of an 8 oz bag of tortilla chips, smashed finely
- 2 tbs lime juice (or liquid Margarita mix)
- 2 tbs corn oil
- 1 tbs honey
- 1 14 oz can Mexican style stewed tomatoes
- 1 tbs cilantro, chopped
- 3/4 lb Jack cheese, sliced - 1/3 inch
- sliced limes and cilantro sprigs to garnish

Preheat oven to 350 degrees. Combine lime juice, corn oil, and honey in small bowl. Brush chicken breasts with lime mixture and roll in tortilla chips. Place coated chicken in small lasagna pan and bake for 25 minutes. In the meantime combine tomatoes and cilantro in another bowl. When chicken is done, pour tomato mixture over, top with cheese, then return to oven until cheese melts. Garnish and serve.

Creamy Chicken Breast Casserole

This recipe is so popular that people continue to request a copy even though it's been nearly eight years since it was featured on our show. Originally called "Center Stage Chicken"

- 1 package cream cheese
- 1 can cream of mushroom soup
- 1 soup can of water
- ½ cup white wine
- 1 package dry Italian dressing
- 4 - 5 boneless chicken breasts

Mix first five ingredients in small bowl. Add chicken breasts to baking pan, cover with cream mixture. Bake one hour at 375 degrees. Serve over wide egg noodles.

Chicken Pepperoni

- ½ lb whole pepperoni stick, diced
- 1 lb boneless, skinless, chicken breast, cubed
- ½ cup flour
- ½ tsp tarragon
- ½ tsp basil
- ½ tsp oregano
- ½ tsp garlic powder
- ½ tsp onion powder
- ½ tsp ground black pepper
- 16 oz can tomato sauce
- 1/3 cup water

Mix together flour and spices. Toss chicken in flour mixture and set aside.
Cook pepperoni in medium pan until most of fat has been rendered. Remove
pepperoni and set aside. Brown chicken in pepperoni fat. Remove chicken
and set aside. Add tomato sauce to pan and de glaze. Stir well. Return
chicken and pepperoni, add water and stir. Cover and simmer 20 - 30
minutes. Add flour to thicken if needed. Serve over hot linguini or
spaghetti.

Chicken Dijon

If you've tried no other recipe in this book, at least try this one. It's the second easiest recipe we ever did. And it's one of the tastiest. I make it for Donna on Saturday nights when she wants something "special". Most of the ingredients are probably in your pantry or freezer right now! Excellent with a chilled, dry Chardonnay.

- 2 - 3 chicken breasts
- flour
- clarified butter
- 2 tbs white wine
- 2 tbs Dijon mustard
- ½ cup heavy cream
- cooked pasta

Dredge chicken in flour. Fry in clarified butter over medium heat 6 - 8 minutes per side. Remove chicken and keep warm. Deglaze pan with wine. Add mustard and stir. Mix in cream. Serve over chicken with pasta.

Chicken Parmesan

- 2 - 3 chicken breasts
- 2 tbs butter
- 1 egg
- ½ cup milk
- ½ cup bread crumbs
- ¾ cup parmesan cheese, grated and separated
- 14 oz can tomatoes, un-drained
- 1 tsp Italian seasoning

Mix egg and milk. Dip chicken in egg mixture then dredge in mixture of bread crumbs and parmesan cheese. Sauté in melted butter in skillet over medium heat, 6 - 8 minutes per side. Remove cooked chicken. Add canned tomatoes and deglaze pan with tomato packing juice. Add seasoning. Spoon tomato mixture over chicken and serve topped with more parmesan cheese.

Ginger Chicken with Jalapeño and Sugar Peas

Some think this is an Asian dish infused with a flare of Mexico – because of the Jalapeño. Truth is, it was likely the Chinese who first introduced us to chili peppers like the jalapeño.

- 4 boneless, skinless chicken breasts
- sprinkle of salt
- Asian style toasted (dark) sesame oil
- 2 inch ginger root, peeled
- 1 jalapeño chili, halved and seeded
- 2 cloves garlic
- 1 carrot, cut into match stick slices (or peel)
- 1 cup sugar peas
- ¾ cup chicken broth
- corn starch
- ¼ cup cilantro, chopped
- dry roasted peanuts, chopped
- cooked noodles (Udon , Ramen, or angel hair spaghetti)

Salt chicken breasts and sauté in sesame oil over medium heat and cook for five minutes. Meanwhile, process ginger root, jalapeño, and garlic together. Add to chicken with sugar peas, carrot, and chicken broth. Turn chicken over, cover and cook until chicken is done. Remove chicken and thicken broth with corn starch (pre mixed with water, soy, or broth). Place chicken over noodles, top with sauce, then cilantro and peanuts.

Apple Crisp Chicken

This recipe originated at the Teresita Pines Lions Camp in Wrightwood. John Bauer and his lovely wife Lynda run the camp, which includes cooking for hundreds of people. I was up there one weekend, and John shared this recipe with me. Here's the story - one weekend they had an unexpected group of 100 show up. All he had in his kitchen was chicken, cheese, and Apple Jack cereal. Thank God he had tons of each! He prepared a satisfying dish that everyone loved. I went home and tried it, the kids loved it. We modified it a bit for smaller crowds.

- 4 boneless, skinless chicken breasts
- 2 oz cheddar cheese, sliced
- ¼ cup bread crumbs
- 1 cup apple flavored breakfast cereal
- 2 eggs
- ½ cup milk
- 2 green apples, cored and sliced into eights
- wax paper
- zip locking storage bags

Pre-heat oven to 375 degrees. Spray medium sized baking pan with non-stick coating (or coat with butter). Prepare wash by mixing eggs and milk in a small bowl. Pour apple cereal in zip locking bag and pound until powder like. Add bread crumbs to bag and mix. Lightly pound chicken between wax paper to even out. Roll each breast around a piece of cheese. Secure with toothpick. Dip in egg wash. Place chicken in bag and coat. Place into baking pan. Cover with apples. Bake uncovered for 35 - 40 minutes

Nacho Chicken

The kids will love this one. It tastes great, and it's fun to make. Flatten the chicken between wax paper – use the bottom of a heavy skillet as your mallet.

- 6 boneless skinless chicken breasts (5oz portions), pounded lightly to flatten and sprinkled with season salt.
- 4 canned whole green chilies
- 6 oz Monterey Jack cheese
- ½ cup butter, melted
- 1 cup tortilla chips, finely crushed

Cut chilies in halve lengthwise. Cut cheese in sticks. Wrap a piece of green chili around the cheese stick. Roll the flattened chicken breast around it the chili.. Tuck in edges so chili and cheese are not visible. Secure with a toothpick. Roll chicken in melted butter and then in crushed nachos. Place, seam side down, in greased pan. Bake, uncovered at 400 degrees for 30 to 40 minutes

Nutty Chipotle Chicken with Ginger Chili Vinaigrette)

*Every time I think of this recipe, I crave it and want to make it immediately.
Once you try it, you'll see what I mean.*

- 1 lb skinless, boneless chicken breast
- ¼ cup green onion, chopped
- 1 cup honey roasted macadamia nuts, roughly chopped
- ½ cup fresh orange sections
- 2 tbs corn oil

Roast chicken breasts in a 350 degree oven for 20 - 30 minutes, or until
done. Cool, then cut into bite-sized pieces. In a medium salad bowl,
combine chicken, green onion, nuts, orange sections, and bell pepper. Serve
with Ginger Chili Vinaigrette.

Ginger Chili Vinaigrette
- ½ tsp fresh ginger, minced
- ¾ tsp Chipotle pepper, chopped
- ¼ tsp onion, chopped
- ¼ garlic, chopped
- 1½ tsp pimientos, chopped
- salt and pepper to taste
- 1 tbs fresh parsley, chopped
- 2 egg yolks
- ¼ cup tarragon vinegar
- ¼ cup fresh orange juice
- ½ cup corn oil

In a blender, combine ginger, Chipotle pepper, onion, garlic, pimientos, a
pinch of salt and pepper, parsley, egg yolks, vinegar and orange juice. Blend
well. Slowly add oil, blend well. Chill before serving.

Grilled Chicken with Strawberry-Kiwi Salsa)

I originally came up with this to serve with salmon (had a bunch of fillets in the freezer and needed to try something different). Donna liked it better over chicken (she's not a big salmon fan). Why not try it each way and keep everybody happy?

- 4 boneless, skinless chicken breasts (4-6 oz each)
- salsa (recipe below)

Grill Chicken over medium-high heat for approximately 8 minutes per side (or until done). Top with salsa.

Salmon Variation:

Liberally sprinkle salmon fillets with salt and pepper. Place fillet skin-side up in heavy skillet over medium heat. Cover and cook 3-5 minutes, or until done. Remove skin, serve topped with salsa.

Salsa
- 1½ cups fresh strawberries, cleaned and halved
- 1 kiwi, sliced
- ½ cucumber, peeled and diced
- ½ red onion, minced
- 1 jalapeno pepper, seeded and minced
- ¼ cup fresh cilantro, chopped
- juice of 3 limes, reserve rind and grate
- juice of 1 orange, reserve rind and grate
- 2 tbs honey
- salt and pepper to taste

Combine all ingredients (including grated rinds). Chill until ready to serve.

Red Chili Chicken

Your guests will say "this is just like what you get in a Chinese restaurant".
Believe me, that's a complement.

- 1 lb chicken breast, boneless, skinless, cubed
- 6 tbs cornstarch
- 1 tbs water
- salt and pepper
- ½ cup vegetable oil
- ½ cup chicken broth
- 2 tsp sugar
- 1 tbs soy sauce
- ½ tsp toasted sesame oil (Chinese type)
- 1 tsp rice vinegar
- 2 tsp sherry
- ¼ tsp ground black pepper
- 3 - 4 dried red chills, seeded
- 2 cloves garlic, minced
- 2 tsp fresh ginger root, minced
- 2 tbs green onions, chopped
- steamed white rice

Salt and pepper the chicken pieces. Toss with 4 tablespoons cornstarch and
set aside. In a bowl, mix stock, sugar, soy sauce, sesame oil, vinegar, wine
and black pepper together. Set aside. In another small bowl, mix 2
teaspoons cornstarch and 1 tbs. water.

Heat wok on high, add oil. When oil starts to smoke, add one third of the
chicken. Cook in batches, tossing to brown, until done. Drain cooked
chicken on paper towels.

When all chicken has been cooked, remove all but 2 tablespoons of the oil in
the wok. Add chilies, garlic, and ginger. Stir-fry 2 - 3 minutes over medium
high heat. Add green onions and toss for one minute. Add stock mixture
and bring to boil. Stir in cornstarch and water mixture to thicken. Return
chicken to coat and heat through. Serve immediately over steamed rice.

Chicken Paprikash

I got so many requests for this during our fifth year. Why? During the 30-second open of our show, there was a shot of me dishing this rich looking sauce over chicken. Viewers just had to know what it was.

Chicken Paprikash is a classic Hungarian dish. This recipe follows tradition by using whole chicken, but you can use 4 or 5 chicken breasts instead.

- 1 whole, large chicken, cut up
- 1 onion, sliced
- 4 oz butter
- 2 tbs paprika
- 14 oz chicken stock
- 1 tbs cornstarch
- 2 tbs water
- 8 oz sour cream
- 8 – 10 oz egg noodles, cooked and drained
- salt and pepper to taste

In large pan over medium heat, melt butter. Stir in paprika. Sauté onions in butter mixture until onions just begin to soften. Remove onions and set aside. Sprinkle chicken with salt and pepper, then add to pan. Brown over medium high heat. Return onions then cover with chicken broth. Cover and simmer one hour.

Remove cooked chicken and onions from pan and set aside. Bring liquid in pan to boil. Combine cornstarch and water in small bowl. Stir mixture into liquid until thickened to gravy-like consistency. Once thickened, remove from heat. Stir in sour cream (don't boil). Place chicken and onions over pasta, cover with sour cream sauce and serve.

Creamy Pesto Chicken with Mushrooms

Pesto is so versatile. It adds so much flavor to fish and poultry. This elegant dish will impress even the most pretentious of food snobs.

- 1 cup fresh basil leaves
- 3 cloves garlic, peeled and left whole
- 2 tbs pine nuts
- 1/3 cup olive oil
- 1 tbs olive oil
- 4 boneless, skinless chicken breasts
- flour
- ½ cup white wine
- 1 tbs chopped garlic
- 6 oz mushrooms, stemmed and sliced thin
- 8 can artichoke hearts, halved
- 2 cups heavy whipping cream
- ½ cup Romano cheese
- salt and pepper
- 12 - 16 oz. fettuccine, cooked and drained
- roasted red bell pepper for garnish

Make pesto: combine basil, garlic cloves, pine nuts, and 1/3 cup olive oil in blender or food processor. Puree until smooth. Set aside.

Pound chicken breasts between wax paper until evenly ¼ inch thick. Dredge in flour. Heat remaining oil in pan over high heat. Add chicken and brown on one side (2 minutes). Turn breasts over., add wine, chopped garlic, mushrooms, artichoke hearts, pesto, and cream. Stir to distribute evenly around chicken. Bring to boil then reduce heat and simmer until cream has thickened (4 minutes). Turn off heat. Remove chicken; add half of cheese to cream mixture and season with salt and pepper.

Add pasta to large serving bowl or platter. Arrange breasts on top. Cover with cream sauce. Sprinkle with remaining cheese. Garnish with roasted red bell pepper strips.

Creamy Margarita Chicken

- 1 lb spaghetti
- ½ cup fresh cilantro, chopped
- 6 cloves garlic, minced
- 2 tbs fresh jalapeno, mined
- ¼ lb butter
- ½ cup chicken stock
- 3 tbs tequila
- 3 tbs lime juice
- 3 tbs soy sauce
- 1 lb chicken breast, diced
- ½ cup red onion, minced
- ½ cup red bell pepper, diced
- ½ cup green bell pepper, diced
- 1.5 cups heavy cream
- 1 lb. spaghetti, cooked

Melt half the butter in large skillet over medium heat. Cook cilantro, garlic, and jalapeno for 5 minutes. Add chicken stock, tequila, and lime juice. Bring mixture to boil and cook down until thick. Set aside.

Marinade chicken with soy sauce for 5 minutes. In separate skillet, melt remaining butter and cook onion and peppers over medium heat for 3 minutes. Add chicken and cook 1 minute. Add tequila mixture and cream. Increase heat until mixture boils and chicken is cooked through (don't overcook chicken). Serve over spaghetti.

Tropical Pineapple Chicken

<u>Tropical Salsa</u>

- 1 20 oz can pineapple chunks, juice reserved
- ½ red bell pepper, diced
- ½ green bell pepper, diced
- 2 tbs green onions, chopped
- 1 tbs fresh cilantro, minced
- 1 jalapeño chili pepper, seeded, deveined and minced
- zest of one lime
- salt and pepper to taste

Save ½ cup of the juice, combine rest of juice and remaining ingredients in bowl.

Remaining ingredients:

- 4 boneless, skinless chicken breasts
- 1 clove garlic, pressed
- 1-2 tbs clarified butter or vegetable oil
- salt and pepper to taste

Prepare salsa and chill. Meanwhile, rub chicken breasts with pressed garlic. Over medium heat, sauté chicken in oil until brown. Turn over; add ½ cup reserved pineapple juice (from salsa recipe). Reduce heat and cover, cook for 8 - 10 minutes or until done. Serve topped with tropical salsa.

Enchiladas Rojas (with White Refried Beans)

Are you tired of the same old chicken or beef enchiladas? Then try this recipe. The pablano chilies and fresh tomatoes give these enchiladas the special kick. The White refried beans are great too!

- 2 - 3 tbs vegetable oil
- 2 - 3 boneless, skinless chicken breasts, sliced
- 1 onion, sliced
- 1 - 2 fresh tomatoes, diced
- 2 Pablano chili peppers, roasted and sliced
- 6 flour tortillas
- 4 oz. Jack Cheese, grated
- 2 tbs cilantro, chopped

Heat oil in skillet over medium high heat. Add chicken and onions. Cook for 3 - 5 minutes. Add tomatoes and peppers. Cook until chicken is done.

Heat tortillas in another dry skillet over medium heat. Spread with White Refried Beans. Top with Chicken mixture, then cheese and cilantro. Serve with White Refried Beans (see below)

White Refried Beans

- 2 - 3 tbs vegetable oil
- ½ cup carrots, chopped
- 2 tbs green onions, chopped
- 2 cloves garlic
- large can white beans, un-drained

Heat oil in skillet over medium heat. Add carrots, onions, and garlic. Sauté until soft, add beans. Let simmer over low heat for 5 minutes. Prepare chicken (above).

Chili Rellenos Casserole

Easier than traditional Chili Rellenos, with the same great taste. Leftovers can be cut into squares and served as an appetizer.

- 1 lb. Jack cheese, sliced
- 1 large can Anaheim green chilies, sliced open, seeded, rinsed, and patted dry
- ½ cup whole milk
- ½ cup flour
- 2 eggs
- 1 tsp baking powder

Preheat oven to 350 degrees. Blend egg, milk, and flour in blender, pour just enough to cover the bottom of buttered lasagna pan. Layer chilies then cheese slices in pan (make at least two layers). Pour rest of milk mixture over top, bake uncovered until brown (45 minutes or so).

Lee's Meat Loaf

- 1 lb lean ground beef
- 1 lb breakfast sausage
- 1 small onion, finely chopped
- 1 clove garlic, minced
- 1 tsp salt
- 1 tsp Dijon mustard
- 1 tsp ground black pepper
- 1 tsp Worchester sauce
- 1 tbs ketchup
- pinch nutmeg
- dash Tabasco
- 2 eggs
- 2/3 cup bread crumbs soaked in milk

In a large bowl, mix meats together. Add all ingredients (except eggs and bread crumbs). Mix together using your hands. Beat eggs lightly and add with drained bread crumbs, mix. Mold into loaf and place in baking pan. Bake at 350 degrees for 1 hour 15 minutes.

Chicken Taco's with Homemade Corn Tortillas

Thanks to our friend Laura for showing me how to make fresh corn tortillas. Freshly made corn tortillas don't need to be fried for tacos. Find the instant corn mesa mix and the wooden tortilla press at most larger Latino markets.

Corn Tortillas
- 2 cups instant corn mesa mix
- 1-cup water
- I gallon sized zip locking plastic bag

Dampen a clean cloth towel and place on plate. Mix corn mesa and water in medium bowl (per package directions). Form balls about the size of golf balls. Place on plate and cover with towel to keep them moist.

Bring heavy skillet or griddle (cast iron is best) to medium heat. Line wooden tortilla press with plastic bag (cut sides of bag to form one large piece). Press mesa balls between plastic in the press. Place in ungreased skillet and cook approximately 2-3 minutes per side. Keep warm in foil or tortilla warmer until all are cooked.

Chicken Tacos
- 3-4 whole chicken breasts
- ¼ cup salt
- 1 cup cheddar or jack cheese, shredded
- 1 tomato, diced
- 1 head lettuce, shredded
- 12 homemade corn tortillas (recipe above)
- taco sauce

Fill large Dutch oven or large pot half-full of water. Add ¼ cup salt. Add chicken breasts and bring water to boil. Once boiling, cover, and reduce heat to low simmer. Cook for 2 – 3 hours. Cool cooked chicken, remove skin, and shred with fork. Discard bones.

Place shredded chicken on fresh corn tortilla. Top with cheese, tomato, lettuce, and taco sauce.

Spicy Meat Loaf

A departure from traditional meat loaf, this recipe includes more spice and Barbecue flavoring.

- 1 tbs unsalted butter
- ½ cup onion, minced
- ½ green bell pepper, minced
- 2 garlic cloves
- 1 tsp fresh ground black pepper
- 1 tsp cayenne pepper
- 1 tsp salt
- ½ tsp cumin seeds toasted and ground
- 1 ¼ lb lean ground beef
- ¾ lb ground pork
- 1 ½ cups dry bread crumbs
- ½ cup barbecue sauce
- 3 tbs sour cream
- 1 tbs Worcestershire sauce
- 1 egg
- milk, as needed
- additional barbecue sauce, optional

Preheat oven to 350 degrees. Mince onion, pepper, and garlic and sauté in butter until soft. Stir in black pepper, cayenne, salt and cumin. Sauté additional 2 -3 minutes. Add remaining ingredients and mix well with your hands. If too dry add milk. Form into loaf and place in loaf pan. Bake uncovered for 40 minutes. Raise oven temperature to 400 degrees and continue baking for another 20 - 30 minutes. Brush with additional barbecue sauce in last 10 minutes.

Ground Beef and Cheese with Mushroom Casserole

"Casserole" is what Donna's family calls this recipe. Apparently it was the only casserole they made. When you taste it, you'll find out why. Make plenty because most of your guests will want seconds .It's also great for the campground, just pre-cook the beef and pasta at home.

- 2 lb ground beef
- 12 oz package small shell pasta, cooked and drained
- 1 can tomato soup
- 1 can cream of mushroom soup
- 1 15 oz can corn
- 1 8 oz can mushrooms
- 1 lb cheddar cheese, grated, separated
- salt and pepper to taste

Brown beef in a Dutch oven or very large frying pan, drain fat. Add remaining ingredients with half of the grated cheese. Mix well. Top with the rest of cheddar cheese and cover. Once cheese has melted, serve.
There will be no leftovers. Good for camping!

Dad's Favorite Casserole

Make this when you're in the mood for a good, old-fashioned dinner.
Nobody is quite sure who's Dad favored this casserole, but we have a feeling
he was not a doctor.

- 2 cups uncooked wide egg noodles, cook and drain
- 2 medium onions, diced
- 1 tbs margarine
- 1 lb ground beef
- 1 cup cottage cheese
- 1 cup milk
- 1 can cream of mushroom soup
- ½ cup cheddar cheese, grated
- 2 eggs, beaten
- 1 ½ tsp salt

Sauté onions in margarine until light yellow, set aside. In same skillet fully cook ground beef. Remove from heat. Return onions and add cottage cheese. In 2-quart casserole dish, layer noodles, then meat mixture, then rest of noodles. Combine milk, soup, and salt. Pour over top.

Traditional Irish Corned Beef and Cabbage

Why wait until Saint Patrick's Day? You can enjoy this hearty dish any time of year. It's simple to make, and everyone seems to love it.

- 2 lbs corned beef brisket, packaged and already seasoned
- 5 - 8 whole red potatoes
- 1 head cabbage cut in fourths
- water

Place corned beef in crock pot (or large pot) and cover with water. Cook on low for about 3 hours. After two hours add potatoes. A half hour later add cabbage. When cabbage is done (soft), drain three ingredients and discard broth. Slice beef. Serve meal with rolls and your favorite Irish spirit.

Friday night Tacos

Tacos taste best when eaten in the living room in front of the TV. Prepare tacos in the kitchen, filling your plate with enough to last until the commercial break.

Meat filling
- 1 lb ground beef
- 1 tbs chili powder
- 1 tbs ground cumin
- 1 tbs garlic powder
- 1 tsp ground black pepper
- 1 tbs powdered (or 2 cubes) beef bouillon
- 1 cup water

Brown the ground beef over medium heat in a large skillet until there are no pink spots. Drain off the fat. Add remaining ingredients. Bring to a boil, then turn down heat. Simmer 20 minutes. Meanwhile prepare filling and shells.

Other filling
- 1 lb cheddar cheese, grated
- 1 head lettuce, shredded
- 1 large tomato, cut up

Shells
- 1 dozen corn tortillas
- vegetable oil

Heat medium sized frying pan over medium. Add enough vegetable oil to cover the bottom of the pan and let heat. Fry each tortilla momentarily then turn over (use tongs). When the tortilla starts getting crispy, it's ready. Place on paper towel to drain.

When everything is ready, fill the shells with the meat, cheese, lettuce, and tomatoes. Top with any taco sauce. I prefer Lee's taco sauce

Lee's Taco Sauce

Tacos just aren't tacos without it. Each family member has a mason jar in their fridge full of "Dad's Salsa"(or "Lee's Taco Sauce" as we renamed it during our seventh season). Great on egg burritos or with tortilla chips.

- 12 tbs apple cider vinegar
- 6 dried red chilies, seeded and re-hydrated (see below)
- 1 medium onion
- 2 cloves garlic
- pinch dried thyme
- 2 tbs ketchup
- 1 tbs salt
- 1 tbs pepper
- 2 – 5 tsp horseradish
- 1 28 oz can tomato sauce

Boil 1 cup of water in a small pan on stovetop, or heat water on high in microwave-proof bowl. Remove seeds from chilies and place in hot water until soft. NOTE: those sensitive to chilies should leave the room during this process, (or you could do this part outside on a camp stove).

Blend vinegar, hydrated chilies, onion, and garlic in blender or food processor until smooth. Add thyme, ketchup, salt, pepper, and horseradish and finish blending. Pour this mixture into a container (quart jar, plastic tub, etc) until <u>half full.</u> Fill rest of container with tomato sauce. Stir well. Will last in refrigerator for several months.

Discada

1 - Tocino que suelte grasa
2 - Puerco (Pork – chopped)
3 - Meat (Beef – chopped) ground
4 - Add chopped onion
5 - Add chopped tomatoe
6 - Add green chile (al gusto)
7 - Mix it + Tortillas for tacos,

Beef Stroganoff

Donna and I have this long-standing, friendly disagreement about whose mother made the best stroganoff. When it came time to feature stroganoff on the show, we couldn't settle on a recipe, so we featured both. Now you can decide.

Beef Stroganoff by Sharon Underwood (Donna's mom)

- 1 pound round steak, cut into ½ inch strips
- 1 10 oz can cream of mushroom soup
- 2 cans water
- ¼ tsp paprika
- 3 tbs butter
- flour
- salt and pepper to taste
- ½ cup sour cream

Dredge meat in seasoned flour. Brown in butter. Remove from heat and add soup, water & paprika. Bring to a boil, stirring often. Simmer for 45 minutes. Stir in sour cream, gently, just before serving. Serve over wide egg noodles or rice.

Beef Stroganoff by Beverly Baker (Jeff's mom)

- 1 lb <u>cooked</u> chuck or seven-bone roast
- 1 cup beef broth
- 1 tsp dried basil
- 1 lb fresh button mushrooms, sliced
- 1 tsp paprika
- salt and pepper to taste
- ½ cup sour cream
- wide egg noodles, cooked and drained

Add stock and basil to large pot, simmer with beef until warmed through. Remove meat, Bring liquid to boil, stir in paprika. Add mushrooms and stir until they are soft. Pull off heat and stir in sour cream. Return beef and stir just enough to warm, serve immediately over cooked wide noodles.

Dijon Beef Stroganoff

Like traditional stroganoff, with a added twist of Dijon mustard. The whipping cream renders a different texture.

- 1 ½ lbs of boneless lean beef
- coarse ground black pepper to taste
- 5 tbs butter, divided
- 1 medium brown onion, chopped finely
- ½ lb mushrooms, thinly sliced
- 3 tbs flour
- 1 cup beef broth
- 1 tbs Dijon mustard
- ¼ tsp ground nutmeg
- ½ cup whipping cream
- 1 lb egg noodles, cooked
- parsley, chopped for garnish.

Cut beef ¼ inch thick and sprinkle meat with a lot of pepper. In skillet melt butter (1 tablespoon) add onion, cook and set aside. In same pan add meat and cook until well browned. Set aside

In same pan add 4 tablespoons butter add mushrooms and cook. Gradually stir in broth. Cook until thick and boiling. Stir in mustard and meat/onion mixture, nutmeg and cream, heat through. Serve over noodles.

Sauerbraten Meatballs

Craving sauerbraten? Don't have two days to prepare it? Is the nearest German restaurant too far away? Don't panic! Satisfy your craving with these quick and easy meatballs. Enjoy with a quality beer and you've got an instant Oktoberfest.

- 1 lb ground beef
- ¼ cup milk
- ¼ cup bread crumbs
- 1/8 tsp ground cloves
- 1/8 tsp ground allspice
- ½ tsp salt
- ½ tsp pepper
- 1 tbs vegetable oil
- 1 cup water
- ½ cup vinegar
- ¾ tsp. ground ginger
- 1 tbs bay leaf
- 4 tbs brown sugar

Mix together beef, milk, breadcrumbs, cloves, allspice, salt and pepper.
Form into balls and place in large, unheated skillet. When all meatballs are complete, turn heat to medium high and brown. Drain fat, and then add water, vinegar, ground ginger, bay leaf, and brown sugar. Cover and simmer ½ hour. Skim fat, remove meatballs and keep warm. Make gravy by adding 2 tablespoons water to mixture and stir. Thicken with flour/water mixture. Return meatballs to coat. Serve over wide egg noodles.

Creamy Dried Beef Chicken

Use the dried beef that comes in a jar. Look for it in the canned meat section of your grocery store. Take advantage of its intense flavor to spice up your chicken. The cream sauce ties in perfectly, and it's a snap to make! The sherry adds a little class, so don't be afraid to serve it on Saturday nights with a little white wine.

- 4 - 6oz. boneless, skinless chicken breasts
- 1 jar dried beef
- 1 cup sour cream
- 1 can cream of mushroom soup
- ½ cup dry sherry

Preheat oven to 300 degrees. Line a 9 x 12 baking dish with some of the dried beef. Take the remaining beef and roll each chicken breast with about 2 pieces of the beef inside. Secure with a toothpick. Place in dish. Mix sour cream, soup, and sherry together and pour over breasts. Cover dish with aluminum foil and bake for 1.5 hours.

Onion Lover Grilled Burgers

I've never found a better recipe for grilled hamburgers. The onion soup is the secret. These are truly the best burgers I've ever made. Note: these burgers cook best over indirect heat using a covered barbecue

- 2 lbs ground beef
- 1 package dry onion soup
- 1 brown onion, chopped
- 2 - 3 tbs teriyaki marinade (thinner variety)
- salt
- fresh ground pepper

Mix beef with onion soup mixture and chopped onions. Form into patties then brush with teriyaki sauce, sprinkle with salt and pepper to taste. Sear directly over coals, then finish over indirect heat (covered grill) until desired doneness.

Carne Asada

Means "meat over fire" in Spanish. This popular Mexican dish is easy to prepare. It's best right off the grill and wrapped in fresh flour tortillas.

- 2 lbs "flap" meat or thin flank steak
- 2 tbs vegetable oil
- ½ tsp dried leaf oregano, crushed
- ½ tsp salt
- ¼ tsp coarsely ground pepper
- ¼ cup orange juice
- 2 tsp cider vinegar
- 2 orange slices, cut ½ inch thick
- four tortillas
- garnishes: fresh cilantro, cheese, green onions, lettuce, sour cream

Place steak in a shallow glass baking dish. Rub oil on each side of steak. Sprinkle with oregano, salt and pepper. Sprinkle orange juice and vinegar over steak. Cover and refrigerate for 8 hours for best flavor.(turning occasionally).

To cook, bring meat to room temperature. Prepare and preheat charcoal grill. Drain meat and discard marinade. Place steak on grill over hot coals. Top with orange slices. Grill 3 to 4 minutes on each side, or until medium. Cook longer, if desired. Serve wrapped in warm tortillas with salsa. Top with fresh cilantro, onions, cheese, etc.

Ramsa (Beef and Cabbage Rolls)

My grandmother, Marie Baker, a German immigrant, arrived in the states as a young girl. Before that, her family lived in a Russian community along the Volga River. This is one of the many family recipes she made for us, They are easy to make and very satisfying.

- 1 box Pillsbury (or any brand) dry roll / pizza dough mix
- 1 lb ground round beef or sausage
- 1 onion, chopped
- 2 cups cabbage, shredded
- flour
- salt and pepper to taste

In a skillet, cook meat with onions. Drain fat, add cabbage and cook just until limp. Prepare roll mix per instructions on box. Use flour and roll out individual patties like a 6" pancake. Spoon some meat mixture to one side then fold over and seal. Bake on cookie sheet per instruction on the dry roll mix.

Tuna Noodle Casserole

*An American classic. You don't have to be in a church basement to enjoy
this one. Teach kids how to make this. It's simple to prepare and delicious!*

- 6 oz dried wide egg noodles
- 2 cans cream of mushroom soup
- 1 soup can filled with milk
- 2 cans tuna
- 1 package potato chips

Preheat oven to 350 degrees. Cook noodles per package directions. Drain
and set aside. Crush potato chips. Butter a 9 x 12 inch casserole dish. Add
a small bit of crushed chips to bottom of dish. In a separate bowl, drain tuna
and mix with soup. Add milk and mix until smooth. Pour noodles into dish,
then top with tuna mixture, then top with rest of crushed potato chips. Bake
for 25 minutes. Let set for 10 minutes before serving.

Red Bell Pepper Pasta

Beware fellow carnivores, this one is remarkably satisfying and may result in sympathy toward vegetarians.

- 2 tbs olive oil
- 1 large onion
- 2 garlic cloves
- 8 medium red bell peppers, chopped or processed
- ½ tsp sugar
- 1 tsp salt
- ½ tsp black pepper
- 1 tbs fresh basil leaves, chopped
- 1 tbs fresh oregano leaves, chopped
- ½ cup white wine
- spaghetti or other pasta

Heat oil in large pan. Chop or process onions and garlic and sauté over medium heat until softened 8 - 10 minutes). Add chopped bell peppers, sugar, salt, and pepper. Cook over medium heat until soft (10 minutes). Stir in basil and oregano, cook one more minute. Remove and cool.

Puree mixture in food processor until smooth. Return to pan and add enough wine to thin the mixture to sauce consistency (so it's not pasty). Reheat and serve over pasta.

Shrimp with Bow Tie Pasta and Peas

If you watched this show, you likely heard the crew making a big deal about the peas. This was their reaction to the seemingly kooky notion that someone could get excited about ordinary peas being served with something exotic like shrimp. Truth is, the peas, pasta, and shrimp compliment each other perfectly in this dish. Try it!

- 10 oz. bow-tie pasta (farfalle)
- 2 tbs olive oil
- 2 tbs butter
- 2 tbs green onions, chopped
- 10 oz. raw medium-sized shrimp, peeled and cleaned
- 1 cup frozen petite peas, thawed
- ½ cup white wine
- 2 tbs fresh basill, chopped
- salt and pepper to taste

Cook pasta per package directions, drain and set aside. Heat oil over medium-high heat in large skillet. Add butter and melt. Add shrimp and green onions. Cook until shrimp for 3 minutes. Add peas and wine. Let cook for another 2 minutes. Top with fresh basil and serve.

Spinach Stuffed Manicotti

Manicotti – always a favorite with the ladies. Why? Because serving stuffed pasta shows that you took some extra time, just for her. She doesn't need to know it's simple to prepare.

- 14 - 16 manicotti shells - boiled for 8 minutes and drained

Sauce
- 2 tbs olive oil
- 1 tsp of minced garlic
- 1 tsp dried oregano, crushed
- 1 tsp dried sage, crushed
- 1 tsp dried rosemary, crushed
- 1 tsp dried thyme, crushed
- 1 15 oz can diced tomatoes (or 1.5 cups fresh chopped tomatoes)

Filling
- 1 box frozen, chopped spinach - thawed, drained, and dried with paper towel
- ½ cup bread crumbs
- 8 oz ricotta cheese
- 2 egg whites

Sauté garlic in olive oil for one minute. Add dried herbs and cook for another minute. Add tomatoes with juice. Simmer for 10 minutes.

Meanwhile mix together all filling ingredients except the eggs. Fold in eggs. Fill manicotti. Pour a little of cooked tomato mixture in bottom of 9x12 lasagna pan. Place filled manicotti in pan then cover with remaining sauce. Place in preheated 350 degree oven for 30 - 35 minutes.

Easy Fettuccini in Clam sauce

Another great one from Jeff Herringer and the firefighters from Station 66 in Chino Hills, CA. You can double or triple this recipe for a large group.

- ¼ cup butter
- 4 cloves garlic, minced
- 2 cans chopped clams (with nectar)
- 1 can cream of mushroom soup
- ¼ cup heavy cream
- 1 tbs fresh parsley, minced
- 8 - 10 oz dry fettuccini

Cook pasta per package directions, drain and keep warm. Melt butter over medium heat in large skillet. Add garlic and sauté for 1-2 minutes. Add soup and cream and heat through. Add clams with nectar, stir until clams are heated. Stir in parsley. Serve over hot pasta

Jeff's Easy Lasagna

This recipe was featured on our first show back in 1995. It's so simple. I selected it because it was always so popular with family and friends, and I knew that anybody could make it.

- 1 lb package "no boil" lasagna noodles
- 1 lb ground beef, browned and drained
- 1 16 oz. jar prepared spaghetti sauce
- 1 lb bag grated mozzarella cheese
- 1 16 oz carton of cottage cheese

Place one layer of noodles in the bottom of a well oiled rectangular lasagna pan. Then add half of the spaghetti sauce, beef, mozzarella, and cottage cheese. Follow with an identical layer. Place in 350 oven for about 45 minutes. Take out and let set 15-20 minutes before serving.

Fresh Veggie Lasagna

A slight variation from traditional lasagna. Lighter, with more veggies.
Good for picnics.

- 8 oz lasagna noodles, blanched, drained and cooled
- 6 oz cottage cheese
- 6 oz mozzarella cheese, grated,
- 2 medium Italian squash (zucchini), halved then sliced lengthwise
- 1 medium white onion, sliced
- 1 cup fresh tomatoes, diced
- 1 tbs dried Italian seasoning
- ½ tsp red pepper sauce
- ½ cup tomato juice
- 2 oz parmesan cheese, grated
- olive oil

Preheat oven to 350 degrees. Oil a medium sized baking pan. Layer bottom with half the lasagna noodles. Top with half the mozzarella cheese and half the cottage cheese. Cover with remaining lasagna noodles. In a large bowl, combine the remaining mozzarella, zucchini, onion, tomatoes, Italian seasoning, and pepper sauce. Mix well then evenly cover lasagna. Pour tomato juice over top. Top with remaining cottage cheese and Parmesan cheese. Bake for 30 – 40 minutes.

South of the Border Lasagna,

- 1 medium onion, chopped
- 1 lb lean sausage
- 3 cups salsa
- 2 tsp cumin, ground
- 2 tbs fresh garlic, minced
- 15 oz can Pinto beans, rinsed and drained
- 12 oz Ricotta cheese
- 4 oz cream cheese, softened
- 1 egg white
- 10 oz frozen chopped spinach, thawed, drained and dried
- 4 - 6 oz. jack cheese, grated
- 1 lb. lasagna noodles, cooked
- ¼ cup parmesan cheese, grated
- fresh cilantro to garnish

Preheat oven to 375 degrees. Brown sausage over medium heat in large heavy skillet. Drain excess fat if necessary. Add onions and stir until sausage is fully cooked. Add salsa, cumin, half the garlic and beans.

In a medium bowl, mix ricotta, cream cheese, spinach and rest of garlic.

In lasagna pan, layer noodles then half of sausage mixture then half of ricotta mixture, topped with half of jack cheese. Repeat. Top with parmesan cheese. Bake covered with foil for 30 minutes then uncover for 10 minutes. Let stand at room temperature until sets up (15 minutes) before serving. Garnish with cilantro.

Range Top Macaroni and Cheese

Each summer, we'd produce a special show aimed at kids that were out of school, bored, and needing something to do. We called that show "Kids in the Kitchen". One year, my daughter Jill came on the show help me make this dish. She was around 10 years old. The Los Angeles Times decided to do a story about our show and came out that day. Jill got her picture in the paper!

- 1 cup cheddar cheese, shredded
- 2 oz butter or margarine
- ¾ cup milk or cream
- chicken broth bullion cube
- 10 oz. package dry macaroni

Cook macaroni per package directions. Drain and set aside. Melt butter in large skillet over medium heat. Add milk and heat through. Crumble bullion cube into milk. Stir until cube is dissolved into milk. Add grated cheddar cheese and stir until cheese melts. Add cooked macaroni and stir.

Tomato Basil Pizza

Another easy gourmet dish. Fresh tomatoes and basil from your garden are best, if available.

- 2-3 medium sized tomatoes, diced
- 1/3 cup Italian salad dressing
- 2 oz fresh basil, finely chopped
- package crumbled feta cheese
- 1 lb package pre-grated mozzarella cheese
- 2 pre-made crusts (Boboli or similar brand)

Marinade first 3 ingredients together for about ½ hour. Preheat oven to 425 degrees – make sure rack is located in top third of oven.

Layer the crust with tomatoes topping, followed by mozzarella cheese. Top with feta. Bake directly on rack for about 10-12 minutes.

Pizza Pot Pie

Note: buy the frozen bread dough one day before you plan to make this. Follow the instructions on the packaging for thawing and raising.

- 4 - 5 Italian sausage links
- 2 cloves garlic, minced
- 1 medium onion, sliced
- 1 red bell pepper, sliced
- 4 oz. mushrooms, sliced
- 12 oz. Marinara Sauce
- 1 loaf frozen bread dough, thawed, raised, and brought to room temperature parmesan cheese, grated

Preheat oven to 350 degrees. Cook sausage links over medium heat in 9 inch cast iron skillet until sausages are fully cooked. Remove, and slice. Leave 1 tablespoon of sausage fat in skillet. Over medium heat add 2 tablespoons garlic and onion. Stir until onions are soft. Return sausage. Add peppers and onions and stir until peppers are soft. Add marinara sauce. Let simmer for 10 - 15 minutes.

In the mean time, portion bread in eight equal pieces. Roll into 6 - 9 inch ropes. Place in cris cross fashion over top of skillet. Place skillet in middle rack of oven for 20 minutes, or until bread turns golden brown. Coat with butter-garlic sauce and sprinkle with parmesan cheese

Butter garlic sauce

- 2 oz. butter
- 1 tbs chopped garlic

Melt butter in another skillet, sauté garlic for 3 - 5 minutes over medium low heat.

Pepperoni Pizza Chili

- 1 cup mozzarella cheese, shredded
- 1 lb Italian sausage, sliced, cooked and drained
- 1-15 oz can kidney beans
- 1-15 oz can of pizza sauce
- 1-15 oz can Italian stewed tomatoes
- 1-8 oz can tomatoes sauce
- 1½ cup water
- 1 package pepperoni
- ½ cup green pepper, chopped
- 1 tbs Italian seasoning
- 1 tsp salt

Stir in all above ingredients except cheese into a large sauce pan. Bring to a boil then simmer for 30 minutes. Serve and top with mozzarella cheese

Chili Hills (Barbara Patton)

One year we held an informal chili cook-off on our block. Over 17 chili recipes were entered. I promised that the winner would come on our show and prepare the chili. The local firefighters came over to judge. This recipe won hands down. Barbara came to the studio and shared her recipe with our viewers.

A few years later, I agreed to participate in the Chino Fire Muster and Chili cook off. I found out at the last minute that the chili had to be prepared, cooked, and ready for judging within four hours. I thought of Barbara's simple recipe. She gave me permission to use it. I was not surprised when it won first place! I love this chili and always try to have some on hand in the freezer. Thanks Barbara!.

- 2 lbs ground sirloin
- 1 head of garlic, peeled and minced
- 1 large brown onion, chopped
- 2 bell peppers, cored, seeded and chopped
- 2 tbs Montreal Steak seasoning
- 1 small can diced green chilies
- 1 package beef chorizo
- 1 small can El Pato tomato sauce
- 1-16 oz can tomatoes, drained
- 1-16 oz can pinto beans, un-drained
- 2 tbs cumin
- 1 tbs chili powder

Brown beef with garlic, pepper and onion. Add chilies, and steak seasoning. When beef is cooked, add chorizo and mix well. Add remaining ingredients, and then mash all. Let cook for about 45 minutes then serve. Even better next day. Makes approximately one gallon.

Texas Style Frito Pie

This is bachelor food at it's finest. After a helping of this, you won't be hungry again for hours. Also good as a simple camping meal.

- 1 bag Frito's corn chips
- 1 onion, chopped
- 2 cups cheddar cheese, grated
- 1 large can chili

Arrange half the corn chips in a baking dish. Top with onion and half of the cheese. Cover with chili. Top with remaining corn chips and cheese. Bake 15 - 20 minutes at 375 degrees. For camping, arrange in Dutch oven or other heavy pot, cover, and then place on BBQ until cheese melts.

Tequila Pork Chops

Surely a different way to enjoy pork chops. Pressing each chop with the cumin seed is the secret.

- 4 center cut pork chops. 1 inch thick, fat trimmed
- 4 oz butter, separated
- whole cumin seed
- 2 cloves garlic, minced
- ¼ cup chicken broth
- ½ cup tequila
- 2 tbs lime juice
- 1 jalapeño chili, diced
- salt and pepper to taste

Press each side of chop with half teaspoon of cumin seed. Heat in a large flat skillet. When hot add half the butter, immediately followed by the chops. Brown on each side (about 5 minute's total). Remove and keep warm. Add rest of ingredients, bring to boil, reduce heat, return chops to skillet and let simmer until chops are done (check with knife to ensure pink is gone from middle). Remove chops again and let sauce cook down until thickened. Serve over chops.

Shrimp Egg Fu Yung

- ½ lb fresh shrimp, shelled and diced
- 1 tsp salt
- 1 tsp cornstarch
- 2 tsp sherry
- 6 eggs
- 1 tsp light soy sauce
- 3 tbs oil (peanut or vegetable)
- ½ onion, chopped
- 1 tbs green onion, chopped
- 4 water chestnuts, chopped
- ¼ cup fresh mushrooms, sliced
- 1 cup bean sprouts

Sauce:

- 1 cup chicken stock
- 2 tbs soy sauce
- 1 tbs cornstarch (mixed with little water)
- pepper to taste

Marinade shrimp in ½ tsp salt, cornstarch, and 1 tsp. sherry. Beat eggs in bowl; add soy sauce, ½ tsp salt, and 1 tsp. sherry. Set aside.

Heat 1 tsp oil in wok or large pan. Stir fry green onion, onion and water chestnuts for 1 minute. Add mushrooms, cook 1 minute. Remove. Stir fry shrimp and bean sprouts until shrimp turn pink and opaque. Let cool.

Add all ingredients to egg mixture . Set aside. Make sauce in wok, add chicken stock and bring to boil. Add soy sauce. Thicken with corn starch /water mixture. Add pepper to taste. Keep warm.

Heat 2 tablespoons oil in another large skillet over medium heat. Spoon egg mixture into skillet and cook 2 -3 minutes on each side until golden brown and egg has set up. Serve topped with sauce.

191

Hot and Sour Soup

This soup is perfect for cold weather. Also good when you're feeling a bit "under the weather".

- 4 medium-size dried mushrooms (shitake or other Asian mushroom)
- ¼ lb boneless lean pork, cut in matchstick pieces
- 1 tbs sherry
- 4 cups chicken broth
- ½ lb chicken breast, skinned, boned and cut in matchstick pieces
- ½ cup sliced bamboo shoots, cut in matchstick pieces
- ¼ pound tofu, drained and cut into cubes
- 2 tbs white wine vinegar
- 1 tbs soy sauce
- 2 tbs corn starch
- ¼ cup water
- ½ to ¾ tsp white pepper
- 1 tsp sesame oil
- 1 egg, lightly beaten
- 2 whole green onions, cut in 1-inch diagonal slices
- salt

Cover mushrooms with warm water, let stand for 30 minutes, then drain. Cut off and discard stems; squeeze mushrooms dry and thinly slice. Combine pork with sherry; let stand for 10 minuets

In a 2 quart pan, heat chicken broth to boiling. Add mushrooms, chicken, pork and bamboo shoots. Stir several times, then reduce heat; cover and simmer for 5 minutes. Add tofu, wine vinegar, and soy; heat, uncovered for 1 minute. Blend cornstarch and water. Add to soup and cook, stirring, until slightly thickened. Turn off heat. Add pepper and sesame oil. Stirring continuously, slowly pour egg into soup. Sprinkle with green onions and salt

Kung Pao Chicken (Family Friendly)

Hotter versions include 4 - 6 hot, dry chili peppers (seeds removed), which would be stir fried with the peanuts.

- 1 tbs cornstarch
- 1 tbs dry sherry
- ½ tsp salt
- 1/8 tsp white pepper
- 1 ½ lbs. Chicken breasts, skinned, cut in bite sized pieces
- 4 tbs peanut oil (vegetable oil okay)
- ½ cup salted peanuts
- ½ cup celery, chopped
- 1 tbs garlic, minced
- 1 tbs ginger root, minced
- 2 tbs green onion, chopped

Cooking Sauce:

In a bowl, combine the following:

- 3 tbs chicken broth
- 2 tbs soy sauce
- 1 tbs white wine vinegar
- 1 tbs sherry
- 2 tsp sugar
- 2 tsp corn starch

Combine cornstarch, sherry, salt, and pepper in a bowl. Stir in chicken to coat. Then stir in 1 tablespoon of the oil. Marinade for 15 minutes. Prepare cooking sauce and set aside.

Over medium heat, heat wok or large frying pan. When hot add 1 tablespoon oil. Add peanuts and cook for 2 minutes. Remove. Add 2 more tablespoons oil, when hot add garlic and ginger. Stir once then add chicken and stir fry until chicken is opaque in center (about 3 minutes). Add celery, green onions, and peanuts to pan. Stir cooking sauce, and then add to pan. Cook, stirring until sauce begins to bubble and thickens. Serve with hot rice.

Shrimp in Red Sauce

- 1 lb uncooked large shrimp, peeled
- 1 tbs peanut oil
- 1 tbs ginger, minced
- 1 tbs garlic, minced
- ½ cup ketchup
- 1 tbs sugar
- 1 tbs dry sherry
- 1 tbs Chinese black bean paste
- 2 tbs green onions, diced
- hot cooked rice

Prepare red sauce: combine ketchup, sugar, sherry, and bean paste in a bowl. Set aside. Heat wok or large frying pan to medium heat. Add oil, when hot add ginger and garlic and stir fry for one minute. Add shrimp and cook until pink and opaque in center (about 2 -3 minutes). Add red sauce just long enough to heat. Top with green onions and serve.

Chinese Style Sausage and Tofu

- 1 tbs ginger, minced
- 1 tbs garlic, minced
- 1 lb package lean breakfast sausage
- 1 package firm or extra firm tofu (sliced into 1" square cubes)
- 1 tbs Chinese black bean paste
- 1/2 cup beef broth
- 2 tbs green onions, diced
- hot cooked rice

Heat wok or large frying pan to medium heat. Add oil, when hot add ginger and garlic and stir fry for one minute. Add sausage and fully cook (until pink and opaque in center). Drain, and then add broth. Stir in bean paste and bring to boil. Simmer until broth mixture has almost entirely reduced. Gently fold in tofu only long enough to heat tofu. Top with green onions and serve over rice.

Szechwan Noodles with Broccoli and Peanut Sauce

- 8 oz. dry linguine, cooked then drained
- 2 cups broccoli florets, steamed and placed in ice water to shock, drain
- 1/3 cup peanut butter
- ½ cup vegetable broth
- 1 tsp soy sauce
- 2 tbs rice vinegar
- 2 tbs safflower oil
- 1 clove garlic, minced
- ½ tsp dry crushed red pepper
- 2 cups cherry tomatoes
- 2 tbs green onions, chopped

Wisk together peanut butter and veggie stock. Stir in soy sauce, rice vinegar, oil, garlic, and crushed peppers. Pour sauce over pasta and stir with broccoli and tomatoes. Top with green onions.

Shrimp Creole

When visiting my sister Barb in Houston, her neighbor Jan gave me this recipe. Jan grew up in Louisiana, where this recipe originated. This was her family favorite. It immediately became one of my favorites.

- 6 tbs unsalted butter
- 1 large onion, halved and thinly sliced
- 1 large green pepper, thinly sliced
- 2 celery stalks, thinly sliced
- 2 garlic clove, thinly sliced
- 1 bay leaf
- 2 tbs paprika
- 2 cups fresh tomatoes (canned ok), chopped
- 1 cup tomato juice
- 4 tsp Worcestershire sauce
- 4 - 6 dashes tobacco sauce
- salt
- 2 - 3 lbs fresh peeled shrimp, cooked

Melt 2 tablespoons of the butter in wide pan and sauté the onion, green pepper, celery, garlic, and bay leaf for 1 - 2 minutes until hot and coated with butter. Add paprika, tomatoes, and tomato juice, stir in Worcestershire and tobacco. Bring to boil and simmer, uncovered to reduce volume and cook vegetables (about 20 minutes). Add heated cooked shrimp and serve with white rice. Garnish with lemon peel or zest.

Red Snapper Fajitas

- 2 tbs fresh lime juice
- 1 tsp lemon pepper
- ½ tsp ground cumin
- 1.5 lbs Snapper fillets, boned and cut into ½ inch strips
- flour tortillas, warmed
- 1 tbs vegetable oil
- 1 red onion, sliced vertically
- 1 red bell pepper, seeded, sliced thin
- 1 green bell pepper, seeded, sliced thin

In a large zip lock type bag, combine snapper with lime juice, cumin, and lemon pepper, marinade in fridge for exactly 20 minutes. Stir fry peppers and onions in oil over medium heat until peppers are limp. Keep warm.

Arrange fish on broiler pan and broil for 4 minutes on each side. They are done when they are white (or opaque) through the middle and flake when tested with a fork.

Wrap fish, peppers, and onion in warmed tortillas and top with pineapple salsa.

Pineapple Salsa

Mix the following then chill for at least an hour before serving;

- 1 cup finely pineapple, chopped
- ½ cup red onion, minced
- 1 jalapeño chili, seeded, minced

Orange Beef Burritos

- 2 tbs. olive oil
- 1 onion, chopped
- 1 green pepper, chopped
- 3 garlic cloves, crushed
- 1 tbs. orange rind, grated
- 2 tsp. ground cumin
- 1 tsp. chili powder
- juice of one orange juice
- 1 lb. cooked beef
- 12 flour tortillas

Bring oil to medium high heat in large skillet. Saute onion, pepper, and garlic until soft. Add orange rind, cumin & chili powder. Add orange juice, stirring until liquid cooks down.

Stir in cooked beef. Serve with heated flour tortillas, top with chopped tomatoes, shredded lettuce, grated sharp cheddar, sour cream, and fresh cilantro.

Margarita Salmon

- 1 tsp lemon rind, grated
- 3 tbs fresh lime juice (or lemon juice)
- 1 tbs tequila
- 2 tsp sugar
- 2 tsp vegetable oil
- ½ tsp salt
- 1 tsp lemon rind, grated
- ½ tsp orange rind, grated
- 2 garlic cloves, crushed
- 4-6 0z salmon fillets (thicker body pieces)
- cooked angel hair pasta or white rice
- lime slices to garnish

Combine ingredients in zip locking bag. Add fish and coat. Marinade for no more than 20 minutes. Preheat broiler. Place fillets on broiling pan and broil 7 minutes or until fish flakes. Baste occasionally with reserved marinade. Serve over hot pasta or rice.

Donna giving direction in the booth.

*Jeff and Donna in a pre-show discussion with
Sir Francis Drake (Will Woods)*

*Nothing goes to waste on the Man in the Kitchen set. Greg
Wyatt, Marit Kams and Glenn Tornhill assuring quality control.*

Jeff transported back in time in this show featuring foods of the Renaissance.

Jeff and Dan relax between takes.

Really Impressive Main Entrees

Fettuccini Alfredo

This is always a favorite. You can fancy it up by adding cooked shrimp or chicken if you want. Serve with warmed sourdough bread, salad, and chilled Chardonnay.

- 3 tbs butter
- 3 cloves garlic
- ½ cup heavy cream
- ½ cup grated parmesan cheese
- 10 - 12 oz. fettuccini, cooked
- fresh parsley, chopped
- 3 tbs parmesan cheese

Melt butter in medium skillet. Add garlic and stir for a few minutes (don't burn). Add cream and stir until steaming. Add parmesan cheese. Toss with warm pasta. Top with parsley and more parmesan cheese.

Fettuccini with White Cheese and Asparagus

Use white sharp cheddar from Vermont or Canada. You can typically find them in delis or the specialty cheese section of your grocery store.

- 10 oz Fettuccini
- 2 tbs butter
- 2 tbs olive oil
- 10 – 12 fresh asparagus, tip snapped off
- 1 large garlic clove, minced
- 3 oz prosciutto
- 2 tbs fresh sage, chopped
- ¾ cup cream
- 4 oz sharp cheddar cheese, grated
- 2 oz Gruyere cheese, grated
- salt and pepper to taste

Cook pasta per package directions. Drain and set aside.

Melt butter with oil in large skillet over medium heat. Sauté asparagus tips for about 5 minutes until tender. Add garlic and prosciutto, cook 1 minute. Add chopped sage and cook another minute. Add cream and bring to boil. Gradually stir in chesses, bringing down heat slightly as cheese melts. Season with salt and pepper. Toss with pasta to coat.

Salmon Carbonara

Carbonara is a popular Italian dish that features a creamy tomato sauce. This recipe is a good way to utilize your leftover cooked salmon. Or simply buy canned salmon.

- 8 oz. linguini pasta, cooked and drained
- 6 slices bacon, diced
- ½ medium onion, chopped
- 3 large garlic cloves, minced
- 2 tsp.dried basil
- ½ tsp dried oregano
- ½ tsp ground pepper
- ¼ tsp red pepper flakes
- 2-14oz cans diced tomatoes, un-drained
- 3 tbs red wine vinegar
- 10 - 12 oz. of boneless, skinless canned salmon
- ½ cup heavy cream
- fresh parmesan cheese, grated

In large saucepan, cook bacon and drain, reserving 2 tablespoons bacon fat. Add onion, garlic, basil, oregano, red pepper, and black pepper. Cook about 5 minutes.

Add tomatoes and vinegar; cook for another 10 minutes to thicken. Stir in salmon and cream, heat through. Serve over pasta and top with parmesan cheese.

Around the World Macaroni and Cheese

We had to come up with a name, and this one fit because the cheeses come from all over the world! Use white cheddar from Vermont or Canada, Gorganzola from the Italian village of the same name and Emmenthaler (commonly known in the states as "Swiss" cheese)

- 16 oz. elbow macaroni, uncooked
- 2 cups whole milk
- 2 bay leaves
- ¼ cup flour
- 2 oz very sharp cheddar cheese, grated
- 2 oz Emmenthaler (Swiss) cheese, grated
- 2 oz fresh Parmesan cheese, grated
- 2 oz. fresh Gorganzola or Blue cheese, crumbled
- 2 tsp dried sage
- 4 tbs melted butter
- 4 slices white bread
- salt and pepper to taste

Preheat oven to 400 degrees. Butter a 9x12 (or near that size) casserole (lasagna) pan. Bring stock pot of water to boil. Add macaroni and cook for no more than five minutes, drain. Spoon macaroni into casserole dish and set aside.

In food processor, pulse bread until fine. Mix in sage. Add melted butter and pulse until well mixed. Set aside.

In small saucepot, bring milk and bay leaves to simmer. Remove from heat and cool (3-5 minutes). Remove bay leaves. Place flour in separate bowl. Slowly stir in some of the milk until flour is thick but runny, and then start adding the runny flour mixture back to the rest of the milk in the pot. Stirring constantly, cook milk over medium heat until milk has thickened. Stir in cheeses until all have melted. Taste and correct with salt and pepper.

Pour cheese mixture over macaroni. Sprinkle bread mixture over top. Bake for 20 minutes, or until breadcrumbs have browned.

Three Cheese Rigatoni

Another rich and tasty cheese pasta dish. This one features French Camembert cheese. It's found at most grocery stores

- 1 tbs butter
- 1 tbs flour
- ½ tsp pepper
- ¼ tsp salt
- 1-12oz can evaporated milk
- ¼ cup white cheddar cheese, shredded
- ¼ cup crumbled Gorgonzola cheese
- ¼ cup Camembert cheese, diced
- 6 cups rigatoni, cooked and drained
- 2 tbs basil, chopped
- ¼ cup Parmesan cheese, finely grated

In a large pan, melt butter over medium heat. Add flour and cook 30 seconds, stirring constantly with whisk. Add pepper, salt and milk. Bring to a simmer, stirring continually. Remove from heat, add white cheddar, Gorgonzola and Camembert cheeses, stirring until cheese melts. Stir in pasta and basil. Once served, sprinkle with Parmesan cheese.

Garlic Pesto Shrimp over Angel Hair pasta

- 8 oz medium shrimp, peeled
- 3 tbs butter
- 6 cloves garlic, chopped and separated
- 5 fresh basil leaves
- 2 tbs parmesan cheese
- 3 oz pine nuts
- 3 tbs olive oil
- 8 oz angel hair pasta, cooked

Prepare pesto by combining basil leaves, 2 - 3 cloves garlic, parmesan cheese, pine nuts, and olive oil in food processor. Puree and set aside.

Melt butter over medium heat. Add 2 - 3 cloves of the garlic and stir. Add shrimp and stir until pink (2 - 3 minutes). Stir in pesto and heat through. Toss with pasta and serve.

Pasta Puttanesca – Harlot's Pasta

It appears that cooking is really the world's oldest profession. I know why this recipe would stay around for the ages. It's quick, spicy, and satisfying.

- ¼ cup olive oil
- 2 tbs butter
- ½ cup onion, chopped
- 2 tbs garlic, minced
- 2 ½ cups tomatoes, chopped
- 2 oz anchovy fillets
- ½ tsp red pepper flakes
- 1 tbs capers
- 1 cup Kalamata olives, pitted
- ½ cup prosciutto, julienne
- cooked pasta

Melt butter in olive oil over medium heat in skillet. Add onion and garlic and sauté until onion is soft. Add tomatoes and simmer 10 minutes. Add anchovies and pepper flakes - cook 1 minute. Stir in capers, olives, and prosciutto just long enough to heat. Add cooked pasta to heat then serve with chopped fresh parsley (optional).

Lasagna Vandewier

Who would expect such a great lasagna recipe from the Dutch? Thank you Audrey Vandewier for sharing this recipe with us. This is the best lasagna I've ever had. Spend an afternoon making this with your friends and family.

Sauce:

- ½ cup olive oil
- 4 medium onions, diced
- 2 cloves garlic, chopped
- 3-14 oz can tomatoes, drained
- 2 tbs chopped parsley
- 6 basil leaves
- 5 6oz cans tomato paste

Brown onion & garlic in oil, add remaining ingredients, simmer 15 minutes.

Meatballs

- 2½ lbs ground beef
- 1½ lbs hot Italian sausage
- ½ cup bread crumbs
- 4 tbs parsley, chopped
- 5 tbs milk
- 2 beaten eggs
- 7 tbs, parmesan cheese
- salt and pepper

Mix ingredients thoroughly and shape into tiny meatballs. Brown in pan with small amounts of olive oil. Add sauce and simmer 30 minutes.

Lasagna

- 1 lb lasagna noodles, cooked
- 2-1 lb mozzarella cheese, grated
- 1½ lb. ricotta cheese
- ½ lb parmesan cheese, grated

Layer, bake at 350 degrees for 20 minutes or until hot through and cheese melted. Makes two full pans.

212

Seafood Lasagna,

- 9 dry lasagna noodles
- 1 tbs butter
- 1 cup onion, diced
- 1-8 oz cream cheese
- ½ cup cottage cheese
- 1 egg, beaten
- 2 tsp dried basil
- ½ tsp salt
- 1/8 tsp ground black pepper
- 2 cans condensed cream of mushroom soup
- 1/3 cup milk
- 1/3 cup dry white wine
- 1 6 oz can crabmeat, drained and flaked
- 1 lb cooked shrimp
- ¼ cup Parmesan cheese, grated
- ½ cup sharp cheddar cheese, shredded

Bring a pot of lightly salted water to a boil. Add pasta and cook for 8 to 10 minutes, drain. Keep separate so they do not stick together. Preheat oven to 350 degree's

In a skillet, heat butter and sauté onion over medium heat until tender. Remove from heat and stir in cream cheese, cottage cheese, egg, basil, salt and pepper. Mix well.

In a mixing bowl, combine the soup, milk, wine, crabmeat and shrimp.

Lay 3 cooked noodles on the bottom of a 9 x 13 baking dish. Spread 1/3 of the onion mixture over the noodles. Then spread 1/3 of the soup mixture over the onion layer. Repeat the noodle, onion, soup layers twice more. Top with cheddar cheese and Parmesan cheese. Bake uncovered in a preheated oven for 45 minutes or until heated through the bubbly.

Pasta Torta

I might have called this "Spaghetti Cake" on the show. It presents well because it actually looks like a two-layer cake! Your friends will love it.

- 4 cups cooked spaghetti
- 2 eggs
- ¼ cup parmesan cheese
- 1 lb. ground beef
- ¼ tsp salt
- ¼ tsp pepper
- 16 oz can tomato sauce
- 1 garlic clove, minced
- ½ cups sour cream
- ¼ cup cream cheese, softened at room temp
- ½ cup green onion, chopped
- 1 ½ cups mozzarella cheese, grated

Preheat oven to 350 degrees. Mix cooked spaghetti, eggs and parmesan cheese. Pat into two 9 inch round cake pans. Bake for 25 minutes. Meanwhile, brown beef and drain. Add salt, pepper, tomato sauce, and garlic. Stir then let simmer for 20 minutes. In a separate bowl, mix sour cream, cream cheese, and green onion. Place one cooled spaghetti pie on plate. Spread cream mixture over top, place second on top. Cover with tomato mixture. Sprinkle mozzarella cheese on top. Serve.

Enchiladas Palos Verdes

We needed to come up with a fancy name for this recipe. Just before the shoot, the crew and I were tossing around ideas. We started naming the ingredients in Spanish. Someone said "verdes" (green). Then somebody suggested "palos verdes". To make a long story short – this name has nothing to do with the recipe.

Green Salsa (Salsa Verdes)

- 1 lb tomatillos (little green tomatoes), husked and cut in half
- 1 cup chicken stock or broth
- 1 jalapeño pepper, seeded and finely chopped
- dash salt

Place tomatillos in sauce pan over medium heat. Add broth until just covered. Add salt and jalapeño. Let simmer until tomatillos have softened (30 - 40 minutes). Puree in blender or food processor. Set aside.

Filling (mix the following together)

- 2 cups chicken, cooked and shredded
- ½ cup Asiago cheese, shredded
- ½ onion, chopped
- 2 tbs fresh cilantro, chopped
- 1/3 cup chicken broth
- ½ cup sour cream
- juice of two limes
- ½ tsp ground cumin
- salt and pepper to taste

215

Enchiladas Palos Verdes (con'd)

<u>In addition</u>

- 8 corn tortillas
- sour cream (garnish)
- sliced jalapeño (garnish)

Oil or butter a 9 x 12 casserole dish. Dip a tortilla in the green sauce and then place some filling in the middle. Roll and place in pan, seam side down. Repeat for remaining tortillas. Cover with remaining sauce. Cover with foil and bake for 20 minutes. Remove foil and bake another 10 minutes. Garnish with sour cream and jalapeños.

Grilled Chicken with Strawberry-Kiwi Salsa

<u>Chicken</u>
- boneless, skinless chicken breast or 4 (4-6 oz salmon fillets)
- salt and pepper to taste

Grill chicken over medium heat for approximately 8 minutes per side, or until done. Top with salsa

<u>Salmon</u>
Liberally sprinkle salmon with salt and pepper. Place filets skin-side up in heavy skillet over medium heat. Cover and cook for 3 -5 minutes, or until done. Remove skin, serve topped with salsa.

<u>Salsa</u>
- 1½ cups fresh strawberries, cleaned and sliced
- 1 kiwi, sliced
- ½ cucumber, peeled and diced
- ½ red onion, mined
- 1 jalapeno pepper, seeded and minced
- ¼ cup fresh cilantro, chopped
- juice of 3 limes (grate rind, 1 tablespoon)
- juice of 1 orange (grate rind 1 tablespoon)
- 2 tbs honey
- salt and pepper to tasted

Combine all ingredients. Chill until ready to serve.

Donna's Favorite Raspberry Chicken

When I offer to cook Donna a special dinner she often requests Raspberry Chicken. Most grocery stores carry the raspberry vinegar.

- 3 – 4 2 lbs boneless, skinless chicken breasts
- 2 tbs butter
- ¼ cup yellow onion, finely chopped
- 4 tbs raspberry vinegar
- ¼ cup chicken broth
- ¼ cup heavy cream
- 1 tbs crushed tomatoes
- 15 - 16 fresh raspberries

Flatten each breast pressing it gently with the palm of your hand. Melt the butter in a large skillet over low heat. Raise the heat, add the chicken and cook for about 3 minutes per side, or until they are lightly colored. Remove from the skillet and reserve.

Add the onion to the fat in the pan and cook, covered, over low heat until tender, about 15 minutes. Add the vinegar and deglaze pan. Raise the heat and cook, uncovered, stirring occasionally, until vinegar is reduced to a syrup spoonful. Whisk in the chicken stock, heavy cream and crushed tomatoes. Simmer for one minute. Return chicken to the skillet and simmer them gently in the sauce, basting often, until they are just done and the sauce has been reduced and thickened slightly, about 5 minutes. Do not overcook.

Remove chicken with a slotted spoon and arrange on a heated serving platter. Add the raspberries to the sauce in the skillet and cook over low heat for 1 minute. Do not stir the berries with a spoon, merely swirl them in the sauce by shaking the skillet. Pour sauce over chicken and serve immediately.

Chicken with Lemon-Caper Sauce

This is Donna's second most requested recipe. The capers, vermouth and lemon juice give it just the right flavor. Serve with a crisp white wine like Chenin Blanc.

- 1 tsp salt
- ¼ tsp pepper
- 4 chicken breast halves, skinned and boned
- 1 tbs olive oil
- cooking spray
- 1/3 cup extra-dry vermouth
- 3 tbs fresh lemon juice
- 1½ tbs capers
- 1 tbs fresh parsley, chopped

Sprinkle 1/8 teaspoon salt and 1/8 teaspoon pepper evenly over chicken. Heat oil in a large nonstick skillet coated with cooking spray over medium-high heat. Add chicken; cook 6 minutes on each side or until chicken is done. Remove from skillet. Set aside and keep warm.

Add 1/8 teaspoon salt, 1/8 teaspoon pepper, vermouth, lemon juice and capers to skillet, scraping skillet to loosen browned bits. Cook until reduced to ¼ cup (about 2 minutes). Stir in parsley. Spoon sauce over chicken.

Chardonnay Chicken

- 4-6 boneless chicken breasts - pounded (use wax paper)
- ½ cup Chardonnay or other dry white wine
- ¼ cup lemon juice
- 6 green onions, chopped
- 2 cloves garlic, pressed or crushed
- butter
- olive oil
- flour

Lightly flour chicken. Melt 2 tablespoons butter with 1 tablespoon olive oil in a large skillet over medium heat. Add chicken and fry until golden brown about 5 minutes on each side. Place in warm (150- 200 degree) oven. Melt 3 more tablespoons of butter to the pan. Sauté onions and garlic. Add wine and lemon juice - simmer on low for 5 minutes. Add chicken to sauce. Cover and simmer for 5 - 10 minutes. Serve with rice and a salad. ´

Braised Chicken in Creamy Bourbon Sauce

- 3 - 4 chicken breasts, boneless skinless
- wax paper
- 1 tbs butter
- 2 tbs olive oil
- ½ onion, chopped
- 2 cloves garlic, minced
- ¼ cup chicken broth
- ¼ cup bourbon
- ¼ cup heavy cream

Pound chicken breasts between wax paper until thinner and somewhat uniform in thickness. Melt butter with olive oil in large sauté pan over medium high heat. Add onions and garlic and stir for 2 minutes. Add chicken breasts and brown (about 3 minutes per side). Add chicken broth and bourbon, let simmer until chicken is done. Remove chicken and keep warm. At this point, the liquid should have reduced by at least one half. Stir in heavy cream. Add salt and pepper to taste. Serve cream sauce over chicken breasts.

Garlic Lover's Shrimp

Regular viewers of our show know that I like to joke about other TV cooking shows in which the audience goes wild every time the host mentions garlic. I insist their set has a lighted applause sign. However, this dish was so fragrant with garlic, the crew was really going nuts as I prepared it on the show. They could hardly wait until the break to taste it.

- ¾ cup olive oil
- 12 cloves garlic, sliced
- 2 lbs medium to large shrimp, peeled and cleaned
- 1 fresh green chili, seeded and sliced thin
- 1 cup clam juice
- juice of 3 limes
- 2 tsp fresh parsley, chopped
- salt and pepper to taste

Heat olive oil in large skillet over low heat. Add garlic and gently stir for three minutes (don't let burn or get too brown). Remove garlic with slotted spoon (leaving oil in pan), place garlic on paper towel and set aside. Increase heat to medium. Add shrimp and chili to pan and stir until shrimp are done (turn pink and opaque through middle). Add clam juice and lime juice to pan and stir. Taste with salt and pepper, serve topped with fresh parsley.

Orange Bourbon Chicken

You'll love this unique twist of Bourbon as an ingredient. Combined with orange and allspice, it's the perfect sauce for chicken.

- 4 skinless, boneless chicken halves
- ¼ tsp salt
- ¼ tsp ground black pepper
- ¼ cup flour
- 3 tbs margarine
- 2 tbs brown sugar
- 2 tbs corn starch
- 1/8 tsp ground allspice
- 1 cup hot water
- ¼ cup orange juice
- ¼ cup bourbon whiskey
- ¼ cup chopped raisins
- 4 slices oranges

Sprinkle chicken with salt and pepper then dredge in flour. Brown in melted margarine over medium heat. Remove chicken and set aside.

Stir brown sugar, cornstarch, and allspice into skillet. Slowly stir in water . Reduce heat and simmer while stirring until thick (about 5 minutes). Stir in orange juice, bourbon, and raisins. Return chicken to skillet and top each breast with orange slice. Cover and simmer for about 30 minutes, or until chicken is done. Serve with sauce. Great over angel hair pasta.

Marmalade Chicken with Cranberries

- 1 tbs olive oil
- 2 -3 boneless and skinless chicken breast halves, pound to ¼ inch.
- 1 egg beaten
- ½ cup breadcrumbs
- ¼ cup Grand Marnier
- ¼ cup orange marmalade
- 1 tsp fresh lemon juice
- ¼ tsp Worcestershire sauce
- ¼ tsp Dijon mustard
- ¼ tsp garlic, minced

Dip chicken in egg then breadcrumbs to coat. Cook in hot skillet with olive oil, about 2 minutes on each side. Remove chicken from skillet and keep warm. Add Grand Marnier to skillet. Bring to boil scaraping up browned bits. Blend in marmalade. Mix in remaining ingredients. Reduce heat to low. Return chicken to skillet. Cover and simmer about 10 minutes, basting with glaze.

Feta Stuffed Chicken Breasts

When the cameras were rolling, I never could get the feta stuffing to stay inside the chicken. It was okay, because it was tasty regardless. Maybe you'll have better luck!

- 2 tbs olive oil, divided
- ¾ cup canned or frozen artichoke hearts (not the kind that's marinated in oil)
- 2 green onions, minced
- 2 oz. feta cheese, crumbled
- 1 tsp Dried herbs de Province
- salt
- pepper
- 4 boneless, skinless chicken breasts
- 1 cup chicken broth
- juice of two lemons
- 2 tsp Cornstarch
- fresh parsley, chopped
- lemon rinds

In heavy skillet over medium heat, sauté artichokes and shallots in 1 tablespoon of the oil for 3 - 4 minutes. Place in bowl and let cool. Stir in cheese, half the herbs de Province. Season with some salt and pepper. Cut pocket in each chicken breast, stuff with cheese mixture. Sprinkle breasts with more salt and pepper.

Add more oil to skillet, add chicken and sauté 5 - 6 minutes per side or until done. Remove from pan and keep warm. Add rest of herbs and broth to skillet. Bring to boil. Combine lemon juice and cornstarch. Add to broth to thicken stirring with a whisk. Return chicken to pan and coat. Garnish with parsley and lemon rind.

Chicken Parmesan with Marsala Mushroom Sauce

This is a delicious variation of the popular "Chicken Marsala". In this dish, the chicken is breaded. I prefer this variation, I hope you will too.

- 3 tbs olive oil
- 2 tbs butter
- 1 cup seasoned bread crumbs
- 1 cup grated parmesan cheese
- chicken breast
- 1 cup flour
- 2 eggs, beaten in med. bowl

Sauce:

- 1 lb fresh mushrooms, sliced
- 4 tbs butter
- 1/3 cup Marsala wine

Combine bread crumbs, seasoning and cheese on plate. Coat chicken with flour, dip in egg, then coat with bread crumb mixture. Chill in refrigerator for at least one hour. Melt butter in middle of skillet, then place olive oil around the butter. Fry chicken until golden brown. Remove and keep warm.

When finished cooking chicken, add rest of butter to pan. Sauté mushrooms, add wine, and then stir until hot. Pour over chicken. Serve with wild rice or hot noodles.

Curry Chicken with Coconut

- 1 lb. chicken boneless, skinless chicken breast, cubed
- ¼ cup unsalted cashews
- ¼ cup vegetable oil
- ¼ tsp mustard seeds
- ¼ tsp cumin seeds
- ¼ tsp. ground coriander
- 1 tbs curry powder
- 1 medium onion, thinly sliced
- 1 tbs fresh ginger root, minced
- 1 clove garlic, minced
- 1 14 oz. can unsweetened coconut milk
- ¼ cup frozen peas
- 2 tbs fresh cilantro, chopped
- 1 cup water
- salt and pepper
- cooked rice

In medium sized skillet over medium heat, toast cashews until they begin to brown, remove from pan, set aside. Lightly season chicken with salt and pepper. Heat oil in fry pan over high heat. Add chicken and stir-fry about 2 minutes. Remove and set aside. Reduce heat to medium.

Have the cup of water handy. Add mustard seeds to pan and stir-fry for one minute (or until they stop popping). Stir in cumin seeds, coriander, and curry powder, cook for another minute. Add onions, garlic and ginger and cook for another 10 minutes, or until onion softens. Add small amounts of water if mixture starts to dry out.

Stir in coconut milk and bring to boil. Reduce heat to low and return chicken to pan, cooking until chicken is done (5 minutes). Stir in peas and cashews, cook for about one minute. Sprinkle with cilantro and serve over hot cooked rice.

Mandarin Chicken with Udon Noodles

Find Udon noodles in the Asian section of most grocery stores

- 6 oz. Udon noodles
- 2 tsp dark (Asian-style) sesame oil
- 2 tsp peanut oil
- 4 boneless, skinless chicken breasts
- salt and pepper to taste
- 1 can mandarin oranges in light syrup (11 oz.), un-drained
- ½ cup chopped green onions
- 1 jalapeño chili (seeded and minced)
- 2 cloves garlic, minced
- ½ cup chicken broth
- 1 tbs light soy sauce
- 2 tsp cornstarch
- 3 tsp water

Cook Udon noodles per package directions (allow 30 minutes for this process). Rinse then set aside.

Heat oils in large skillet over medium high heat. Lightly season chicken with salt and pepper then brown chicken for about 3 - 5 minutes per side. Meanwhile drain mandarin oranges, save syrup. When chicken is browned, put half the syrup in the pan along with the oranges, onions, jalapeño and garlic. Let simmer uncovered for another 6 - 8 minutes, or until chicken is done.

Remove chicken and keep warm. In a medium bowl, mix broth, soy sauce, and remaining orange syrup. Stir into liquid in pan and bring to boil. In small bowl, mix cornstarch and water. Stir into sauce to thicken. Serve chicken on noodles covered with sauce.

Crispy Orange Beef

Be careful when using your wok to deep fry. For safety - ask the little ones to leave the kitchen while you cook the beef. When it's ready, invite them back in because they'll love the orange sweetness of this popular Chinese dish.

- 1 lb flank steak
- green onions, chopped
- 2 tsp. fresh ginger root, minced
- clove garlic, minced
- dried orange peel pieces (about 1 x 2 inches each)
- ½ cup peanut oil (or vegetable oil)

Marinade
- egg white
- 1 tbs corn starch
- 1 tbs dry sherry

Seasoning sauce
- 2 tbs dry sherry
- 2 tbs soy sauce
- 2 tbs sugar
- 1 tsp vinegar
- 1 tsp sesame oil

Cut beef into thin strips, roughly 1 by 2 inch. Marinade (refrigerated) for at least one hour, up to 8 hours.

Add oil to wok and deep fry marinated beef over high heat. Drain beef on paper towels and remove oil from wok. Place wok back on high heat and add green onions, ginger, and garlic. Stir-fry for about 30 seconds, stir in orange peels then add seasoning sauce. Return the beef to the sauce and stir fry for 30 to 60 seconds. Serve with steamed rice.

Crepes with Mu Shu Chicken

Crepes

Tips for perfect crepes: non-stick skillet, good rubber spatula for lifting the cooked crepe out, and quick distribution of the batter over the skillet before the crepe takes form.

- ½ cup all-purpose flour
- ¼ tsp salt
- ¾ cup milk
- 2 large egg whites
- 1 large egg

Combine flour and salt in bowl. Combine milk, egg whites, and egg in another bowl and whisk. Gradually add to flour mixture, stirring with whisk until smooth. Pour into non stick skillet over medium low heat that has been LIGHTLY buttered (the less the better). Tilt pan in all directions to cover bottom. Let cook for 2 minutes, then turn with rubber spatula. Cook for 1 minute.

Mu Shu Chicken (Stir Fry filling for Crepe)

Make sure all ingredients are cut into the smallest pieces possible - this way they cook quickly.

- 1 lb chicken breast, sliced into small strips
- 1 tbs peanut oil (vegetable oil okay)
- 1 tbs garlic,minced
- 1 tbs ginger root, peeled and minced
- 1 red pepper, cored, seeded, and sliced thin
- 1 medium onion, sliced thin
- 2 cups broccoli, chopped up into small pieces
- 1 carrot, grated
- 2 tbs green onions, chopped

Crepes with Mu Shu Chicken (con'd)

<u>Chicken marinade</u>

- 1 tbs sugar
- 1 tbs soy sauce (we used Tabasco brand, it was good)
- 1 tbs rice vinegar
- 1 tsp ground white pepper

<u>Condiments</u>

- Hoisan sauce (also known as Chinese barbecue sauce)
- Plum sauce
- Black bean garlic sauce/paste

Marinade chicken for at least 20 minutes (prepare vegetables during this time). Heat wok to medium, add oil and let heat for a few moments. Add garlic and ginger, stir constantly. Turn heat all the way up and add chicken - cook halfway (about 3 minutes). Add onion and cook for another minute. Add more oil if bottom of wok is drying out. Add rest of vegetables and cook, stirring constantly until broccoli is done.

How to serve: Spread your choice of Chinese condiments (noted above) on crepe (or Mandarin pancake, or heated flour tortilla). Spoon chicken/vegetable stir fry next. Wrap up like burrito and eat by hand, or use a fork if you're in a hoity toity mood.

Elegant Beef Filets

This dish was resurrected from a 1970's cookbook. I wanted to prepare this dish on the show wearing a fake afro wig, but the crew talked me out of it. It's actually great tasting as well as fun to prepare . I recommend buying an entire tenderloin from a meat market. That way you can cut it yourself and leave a little fat on the steak.

- 6 1.5 inch beef tenderloin steaks
- 6 large Portabello mushrooms, gills removed, stems reserved and minced
- 1 extra Portabello mushroom, minced
- 2 tbs butter
- aluminum foil

Sauce

- ½ cup mushroom (from above), minced
- ½ cup green onions, minced
- 4 tsp. cornstarch
- ½ cup beef broth
- 1 cup red wine
- 2 tbs parsley, chopped
- salt and pepper to taste

Preheat oven to 400 degrees. Brown steaks quickly in butter in heavy skillet. Remove and place on foil squares. Top with mushroom cap. Add minced mushrooms and stir until mushrooms appear done. Stir in remaining ingredients. Mix cornstarch with a little water or broth, then add to thicken sauce.

Spoon sauce over steaks and mushroom caps. Seal and place in oven for 10-12 minutes (longer for well done). Serve immediately

Beef Tenderloin en Croute

- 1 beef tenderloin (3 to 4 pounds)
- 1 17¼ oz package frozen ready-to-bake puff pastry sheets
- ½ lb mushrooms, finely chopped
- 2 tbs margarine
- 1 8oz container soft cream cheese with herb and garlic
- ¼ cup seasoned dry bread crumbs
- 2 tbs Madeira wine
- 1 tbs fresh chives, chopped
- ¼ tsp salt
- 1 egg, beaten
- 1 tbs cold water

Heat over to 425 degrees. Tie meat with string at 1-inch intervals, if necessary. Place meat on rack in baking pan. Roast 45 to 50 minutes on until meat thermometer registers 135F. Remove from oven; cool 30 minuets in refrigeration: Remove string.

Thaw puff pastry sheets according to package directions

Cook and stir mushrooms in margarine in large skillet 10 minutes or until liquid evaporates. Add cream cheese, bread crumbs, wine, chives and salt; mix well. Cool

On lightly floured surface, overlap pastry sheets ½ inch to form 14x12 inch rectangle; press edges firmly together to seal. Trim length of pastry 2 ½ inches longer than length of meat. Spread mushroom mixture over top and sides of meat. Place meat in center of pastry. Fold pastry over meat; press edges together to seal. Decorate top with pastry trimmings, if desired. Brush pastry with combined egg and water. Place meat in greased pan Bake 20 to 25 minutes or until pastry is golden brown. Let stand 10 minutes before slicing.

Olive Lover's Steak

Do you love olives? I mean, really LOVE olives. Did you ever finish a whole can all by yourself? If so, you'll dig this recipe.

- 2 lean steaks (filet mignon, porterhouse)
- 1 - 2 tbs vegetable oil
- 12 oz olives (black, green, kalamata, or combination of all), minced
- 4 oz pine nuts
- 2 cloves garlic, minced
- ¼ cup white wine
- ¼ cup beef broth
- ½ tbs corn starch mixed with 1 tbs water

Preheat oven to 150 degrees. Heat oil in medium sized skillet over medium high heat. Place steaks in skillet and grill for 8 - 12 minutes (depending on desired doneness). Turn every three minutes

Remove cooked steaks and keep warm in oven. Add garlic, pine nuts and olives to skillet. Stir for 2 minutes. Add wine and broth, bring to boil. Reduce heat and simmer for 5 minutes. Add cornstarch mixture to thicken. Serve over steaks.

Stacked Green Enchiladas

My friend Bob Gonzalas visited our show and prepared this dish. It's simple, tasty, and festive! Thanks Bob!

- 12 corn tortillas
- 1/3 cup vegetable oil
- 14 oz can green enchilada sauce

Fillings:

- Cooked, shredded chicken breast
- Cheddar cheese, shredded
- Jack cheese, shredded
- Green onions, chopped
- Lettuce, shredded
- Celery, chopped
- Black olives, sliced

Heat some enchilada sauce in medium sized skillet. In another medium sized skillet, heat oil. Fry corn tortillas on each side until limp, then carefully dip in enchilada sauce. Place tortilla on plate, top with fillings of your choice, then repeat for at least 3 layers.

New Mexico Beef Fajitas

Marinade:
- 1/3 cup fresh cilantro, minced
- juice of 3 limes (1/3 cup)
- ¼ cup water
- 1 tbs dried oregano
- 1 tbs ground cumin
- 1 tsp dried, crushed red pepper
- 6 garlic cloves, crushed

Beef/onion:
- ½ medium onion, sliced
- 1 lb flank steak, cut across the grain in thin strips

In small bowl, combine marinade ingredients. Pour half of mixture in zip locking plastic bag. Add onion and beef. Combine well and chill for no more than 45 minutes. Set aside remainder of marinade.

Remaining ingredients:
- 1 cup red bell pepper, sliced thin
- 1 cup yellow squash, matchstick-cut
- 1 cup zucchini, matchstick-cut
- 1 cup corn kernels
- vegetable oil
- 6 flour tortillas, warmed
- 2 fresh tomatoes, diced
- sour cream

Drain marinade from beef/onion mixture. Heat in large skillet on high heat. Add beef/onion mixture and fry for 2 minutes or until beef is mostly brown. Remove and keep warm. Add 2 tablespoons oil to pan. Add bell pepper, squash and zucchini. Fry until limp (2-3 minutes). Add unused, reserved marinade and bring to boil, and then stir in corn. Cook additional 1 – 2 minutes. Return meat to skillet and stir just long enough to heat through. Serve wrapped in warm flour tortillas topped with fresh tomatoes and sour cream.

Rick's Spicy Shrimp with Avocado in Flour Tortillas

My cousin Rick Hale came up with this one. It's so good! The avocado and sour cream cool the fire. Great with an ice cold Henry's.

- 1 tsp paprika
- ¼ tsp cayenne
- ¼ black pepper
- ¼ white pepper
- ¼ thyme
- ¼ basil
- ¼ oregano
- ¼ salt
- 2½ lb. peeled uncooked medium-large shrimp, rinsed, then dried with a paper towel
- 6 oz sliced onion
- 1 clove garlic, chopped
- clarified butter or olive oil for sauté

Mix all spices together and toss with dry shrimp. Sauté onion and garlic over medium heat until tender. Shrimp until pink and opaque. Return onion and garlic to pan and toss. Serve immediately, wrapped in fresh flour tortilla with white rice, avocado, and sour cream!

Baked Feta with Shrimp

A good reason to run out and buy some individual baking dishes – like the ones they use in restaurants. Seriously, this just might be the dish to turn your image around. It presents well, and it's scrumptious.

- ¾ lb medium shrimp
- ¼ cup onion, sliced
- ¼ cup olive oil
- ¼ cup dry white wine
- 2 cups tomatoes, peeled and chopped
- 1 tbs fresh parsley, minced
- salt and pepper to taste

Preheat over to 350 degrees. Sauté onion in olive oil until soft. Add wine, tomatoes, parsley, salt and pepper. Cover and simmer until mixture thickens (appox. 40 minutes). Spoon half of sauce into individual baking dishes. Then layer shrimp. Spoon remaining sauce over shrimp. Top with Feta. Bake 20 – 30 minutes or until shrimp is done.

Shrimp with Feta and Arrabbiata Sauce

This dish features shrimp, but you can serve the Arrabbiata sauce with many things. I like it because it's a quick sauce that tastes like you spent all day making it.

Arrabbiata Sauce

- 2 tsp olive oil
- 1 cup onion, chopped
- garlic cloves, minced
- 1 cup dry red wine
- 1 tbs sugar
- 2 tbs fresh basil, chopped
- 1 tsp dried crushed red pepper
- 2 tbs tomato paste
- 1 tbs lemon juice
- 1 tsp dried Italian seasoning
- 1 tsp black pepper
- 1 14oz can tomatoes, diced and un-drained
- 1 tbs fresh parsley, chopped

Heat oil in a saucepan on medium high heat. Add onion and garlic, sauté for 5 minutes. Add all ingredients except for parsley. Bring to a boil and reduce heat to medium and with pan uncovered, cook for 15 minutes. Add parsley at end.

Shrimp with Feta

- 1 tsp olive oil
- 24 medium shrimp, peeled and deveined
- 1 tbs lemon juice
- 8 oz linguini, cooked and drained
- cups Arrabbiata sauce
- ¼ cup crumbled feta cheese

Heat olive oil in a large nonstick skillet over medium heat, until done. Drizzle shrimp with lemon juice and set aside. Place linguini on a platter and cover with Arrabbiata sauce. Top with shrimp and feta cheese.

Sea Bass Provincial

Specialty retail stores will typically carry flash frozen Chilean sea bass.

- 2 sea bass steaks, 6 - 8 oz. each
- 2 tbs olive oil
- 1 clove garlic, minced
- 2 cups tomatoes, diced
- 1/3 cup Kalamata olives, sliced
- 2 tbs chopped parsley
- ¼ cup water
- 1 tbs capers
- juice of two lemons (grate rind and reserve)

In skillet over medium high heat, sauté garlic in olive oil. Stir in tomatoes, olives, parsley, water and capers. Simmer for 5 minutes. Place sea bass on tomato mixture, cover, reduce heat and let simmer 10 minutes (or until fish is done). Remove skin. Serve fillets topped with sauce. Garnish with fresh parsley and lemon rind.

Thai Shrimp with Mushrooms

- 12 oz. unsweetened coconut milk
- ¼ cup dry white wine
- 2 tbs cornstarch
- 2 tbs water
- salt to taste
- 2 tsp Lumpia sauce or Asian chili sauce (optional)
- 2 lbs medium shrimp, shelled, washed and pat dried
- ½ lb button mushrooms, stems removed and halved
- 2 tbs peanut oil
- 2 tbs butter
- 2 tbs garlic, minced
- ½ cup fresh basil, chopped
- ½ cup green onions, chopped
- 2 tbs lime juice

Prepare sauce by combining coconut milk, wine, and chili sauce. Chill until ready to use.

Heat wok or large skillet over high heat. Add oil and butter. As butter just melts (and before it starts to burn) add garlic. Stir for a moment then add shrimp. Cook shrimp until pink (2-3 minutes). Add mushrooms, basil, and green onions, stir for a moment then add milk mixture. Bring to low boil. In a small bowl mix 2 tablespoons cornstarch and water and add to skillet to thicken milk. Stir in lime juice. Serve over thin noodles or rice.

Jeff took this photo of the crew from his perspective. Pictured left to right: Dan Underwood, Anthony Sarinana, Lee Underwood, Marit Kams, Josh Thompson.

Jeff and Donna Baker

Dan's Desserts

1) Peaches Bellini? → OPEN DRINK
Peaches → Sweet ⎫ blender
1 tbp Simple Syrup ⎬ Batidora → ①
Ice ⎭ → Sugar + Water (Boiled)
Amaretto little
bit

① → Mix with Cold Champage with
espuma

espuma (brinkles)
yellow

SNACK

① Shrimp + Crab oil   Salt + Pepper
② Salt   ↓
③ lemon   ←———   Shrimps
                    Cook in
                    1-2 minutes → Cool them
                                          down on Filter

Unsalted butter → batir + Cream
    + 1/2 lemon   cheese
        + Pepper + Salt + "Mais" + Cherry 1 tbs
    Fridge   bread
                                             with
                                             butter
                                    243 Product

① Chicken breast → Olive oil
        → "Escence"
        → Grill it
          → Escence

② Pending pasta + Salt.
    Put the lid on it
    Pasta → ~~xxxxxx~~.

③ Pesto (Steam it a little
            bit).

"lettuce"/ Food Procesor.
    ("Arrubla") + Pastli (Pereji: !?)
            + Walnuts
            + Garlic (Pesty
            + ~~Parmesan~~ cheese.
Toss it in cool water + Lemon
    with ice.   or wine
                        → Run the
                        Processor
                        When it porrs
                        (Olive oil).
                        3 tbsp (3-5)
        Small
Sliced Tomato (Salted)
  Black Olives
Cream Cheese + Fresh Pepper.

Turkey/Chicken/Sliced | Salad
Pasta → Mixed | with
Pesto | fetta cheese

Cherries Jubilee

- 1 20 oz can dark sweet cherries
- 1 tbs of corn starch dissolved in 2 tbs water
- ½ tbs orange zest
- 2 oz brandy
- 1 pint vanilla ice cream

Drain the cherries, reserving the juice. Combine one cup of juice with cornstarch mixture in heavy pre-heated skillet. Stir and bring to boil. Add orange zest. Turn down heat. Pre heat rum in separate pan - WARM ONLY - do not boil (150 degrees is ideal). Pour rum on cherries then carefully ignite. When flame dies, ladle the cherries over ice cream.

① 1cup Water + ½ cup Sugar + Citrus "peel" + Ginger Slied peeled.

② Mango to blender
+ ⅓ Cup Orange Juice
+ Sugar (depending on how sweet is fruit)
+ A little bit of vodka (1½ tbs).
+ Blend it;

③ All Fruits (small cuts)
bananas, mango, papaya, orange
+ Kiwi + Pineapple + Comcumbers.
+ Passion fruit (just the juice)

245

Pears Flambé

- 3 tbs butter
- 1 cup sugar
- 2 lbs pears, cored and sliced ¼ inch thick
- ¼ cup brandy
- 1 pound cake -- ¼ inch slices
- 1 quart vanilla ice cream
- 1 cup pecans (candied or spiced)
- ¼ cup powdered sugar
- 1 pinch salt
- ½ cup chocolate syrup

In a large skillet, melt butter over medium heat. Add sugar and with a wooden spoon, stir sugar until it dissolves. Continue to stir until sugar starts to caramelize (4-6 minutes). Add pears and a pinch of salt. Continue to sauté' 4 minutes, remove pan from heat and carefully pour brandy into skillet.

Let brandy warm up a little and then light to flambé pears (be careful!!!!) Shake pan until flame dies out, set aside. Place a scoop of ice cream in between two pieces of pound cake and place in middle of serving plate. Spoon the pears over the ice cream sandwich. Garnish with pecans, powdered sugar and drizzle chocolate over everything.

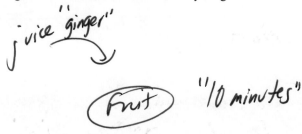

juice "ginger"

"Fruit" *"10 minutes"*

Banana's Foster

This flamed dessert was invented at Brennan's Restaurant in New Orleans in the 1950s. It was named after Richard Foster who served as vice chairman of the Vice Committee in charge of cleaning up the French Quarter.

- 4 tbs butter
- 1 cup brown sugar
- ½ tsp cinnamon
- 4 tbs banana liqueur
- 4 bananas, cut in half lengthwise, then halved
- ¼ cup rum
- 4 scoops vanilla ice cream

Melt the butter in a heavy skillet. Add the sugar, cinnamon and the banana liqueur and stir to mix. Heat for a few minutes and place the halved bananas in the sauce and sauté until soft and slightly browned. Add the rum and allow it to heat well; then tip the pan so that the flame from the burner causes the sauce to light. First lift the bananas carefully out of the pan and place four pieces over each portion of ice cream and spoon the hot sauce from the pan over the top.

247

Crème Brulee (Burnt Cream)

You can find chef's torches at most specialty food equipment stores.

- 9 egg yolks
- 3/4 cup sugar (fine grain)
- 1 quart heavy whipping cream
- 3 inch vanilla bean
- raw sugar

Preheat oven to 300 degrees. Mix egg yolks and sugar until smooth and pale yellow in color (color may vary; just make sure to mix well). Cut the vanilla bean in half. Then cut the bean down the middle and open up. With a knife, scrape out the seeds. Repeat with other half.

In a medium saucepan mix the vanilla seeds and cream.. Under low heat, bring cream to a slight boil. At the moment you start to see bubbles forming, take off heat.

In small amounts, pour cream into egg mixture. Mixing with a whisk, constantly. Keep doing this until all the cream is incorporated in the egg mixture (you do not want to prematurely cook the eggs). Pour mixture into 6- 6 oz. ramekins, about 3/4 full. Place ramekins in a baking pan (13x9x2). Pour hot water in the pan until it reaches half way up the ramekins. Bake 40-50 minutes or until the outer edge of the custard is slightly firm. Cool at room temperature and then refrigerate. *OR beef roast*

When the custard is cold, pour 1 tablespoon of raw sugar in each ramekin. Using a torch, burn the sugar until it becomes light brown. If you don't have a torch, use your broiler. Watch it very carefully, as you know sugar burns quickly. Serve immediately or chill to serve later.

Pork tenderloin

Lettuce - Beer

① 4 mins
roll it and tight it 165c

Bacon cutted
Oil
Onions
Malassa
Garlic
Red Pepper

② Add lettuce
③ Add beer
④ Add Rice - Vinegar

salad pork
⑦ season
⑧ pan 20 min + Rest
⑨ Untight with

248

Ice Cream Cookies

When freezing cookies, use wax paper over a flat surface like cardboard or cereal box.

- 1 cup semi sweet chocolate chips
- 2 pints of your favorite ice cream
- large zip locking bag
- your favorite home made cookies (peanut butter, oatmeal, chocolate chip, etc.)

Prepare your favorite cookie recipe. Let cool. Spoon 2 tablespoons of ice cream onto half of cookies. Top with remaining cookies forming a sandwich. Freeze for 5 minutes. Place chocolate chips in zip locking bag. Microwave until melted. Snip small hole in corner of bag, drizzle chocolate over frozen cookies. Freeze again until ready to serve.

① Turkey / Liver with Teethsticks and Bacon

② Flower + ½ egg

③ Olive Oil

WITH

① Apples sliced, sugar + butter + water

② Blender → over the baby spinachs

⑩ Onion + Remaining pan
→ ½ cup of flower + chicken Caldo

Brownbeans + Rice + Pork Tenderbin + Gravy

"[ ]" + Beans

bread

Corn

249

Toffee-Coffee Dessert

- 1 10 3/4-oz loaf angel food cake
- 1 tbs instant coffee granules
- 1 tbs hot water
- 1 tsp vanilla extract
- 4 cups vanilla ice cream, softened
- 5 5/8 oz chocolate-covered toffee candy bars (4 bars), crushed
- 2 tbs Kahlua or other coffee-flavored liqueur
- 1 8-oz tub frozen whipped topping, thawed

Cut cake into ½ inch slices. Arrange cake slices, overlapping, in bottom of a 9-inch spring form pan; set aside. Combine coffee granules, hot water, and vanilla in a medium bowl; stir well. Stir in yogurt and crushed candy bars.

Spread yogurt mixture over cake slices. Gently stir the Kahlua into whipped topping, and spread over yogurt mixture. Cover and freeze for 8 hours or until firm. You might want to top it off with some hot fudge and whipped cream

Sweet Potatoe Pay

Vanilla
cinammon
groundginger
sweet potatoes
1 eggs
sweet potatoes 50min 350F°

— 4 eggs in a bowl Mix them
— Add 'sugar brown sugar
— Light Carrol + Vanilla

+ wheep cream + chocolate Perdish.
egg mixture Sweet potatoes
nuez
350° — 55min

pay already done

Berries with Butterscotch-Amaretto Custard Sauce

- 1 tbs butter
- ½ cup packed light brown sugar
- 1 cup evaporated milk
- 1 2/3 cups milk
- 2 tbs sugar
- 2 tbs cornstarch
- 1/8 tsp
- salt
- 3 large egg yolk
- 1 tbs amaretto (almond liqueur) or 1 tsp water and a drop of almond extract
- 6 cups berries (your pick) mint leaf (optional)

Melt butter in a medium saucepan over medium heat. Add brown sugar; cook 2 minutes, stirring constantly with whisk. Bring to a boil and cook for 30 seconds, stirring constantly. Remove from heat.

Heat milk in a heavy saucepan over medium heat until tiny bubbles form around edge. Remove from heat. Do not boil.

Combine sugar, cornstarch, salt, egg yolks in a medium bowl. Stir with a whisk until smooth. Stir in hot milk and 3/4 cup of evaporated milk. Add to brown sugar mixture

Bring to a boil over medium heat; cook until thick, stirring constantly. Remove from heat; cool to room temperature. Stir in amaretto. Pour sauce into bowl, cover and chill.

Place cleaned berries in a serving bowl and pour custard sauce over berries.

Mud Pie

You've had this indulgent dessert at restaurants. Did you ever try making it yourself? Now's the time!

- ½ gallon chocolate ice cream, softened
- 16 oz chocolate fudge topping
- 1 large Cool Whip, softened
- 1 chocolate pie crust (deep dish if avail.)
- box chocolate cookie crumbs

Preheat oven to 375. Bake crust for 5 minutes and cool. Take about 1/2 the ice cream and spread it in the crust. Freeze for 45 minutes or until hard. On top of the first layer, spread fudge topping. Freeze for 30 minutes or until hard.

On top of fudge layer, spread remaining ice cream. It will start to look like a mountain. Freeze until hard. Take cool whip and stir in 1/4 cup of cookie crumbs. Then spread over pie. Use has much as pie will hold. Sprinkle more cookie crumbs on top and freeze for 4-6 hours.

Pork loaf

- Jamón en cuadritos chiquititos
- Lean Poark rebanadito desmenruado
- 3 huevos
- Pan Molido
- Sal No
- Pimiento Morrón Rojo
- Tereji s (Parsley)
- Pepper / Garlic/Cebolla
Greby

Horno 350°C - 1h   Durazno - Mermelada
Miel
252. 160°C   Mostaza
infierno

Blueberry Fool

- 2 cups fresh blueberries, stems removed and rinsed
- 1/3 cup sugar
- 1 ½ cups heavy whipping cream
- 4 tbs butter
- 1 tbs Chambord liquor

In medium saucepan, melt butter. Once butter melted add blueberries and sugar. Cook over medium heat for 15 minutes, stirring occasionally. Take off heat and cool completely. Once cool, mash the blueberries with a fork until all are broken. Take off heat. Add Chambord and stir. Whip heavy cream into soft peaks. Fold blueberry mixture into whipped cream. Chill until ready to serve. Serve in a chilled wine goblet and top with more blueberries and whipped cream. You can also float a little more Chambord over to top and garnish with a mint leaf.

Smash Potatoe

Pelar papas -y cortar
Agua fria
Calientas.
Fork-tender.
Tiro el agua y dejo un poco
lo dejo y cuando trono la papa ahi
empeso con mantequilla, crema
y las machaco

Le puso el Sausage en cuadritos
en zanaherias.

Pastelov
papas → graby

Crispy Apple Bake with Cheese and Ice Cream

- 5 cups apples, sliced
- ½ cup water
- 1 tsp cinnamon
- 1 tsp lemon juice
- 1 cup sugar
- 3/4 cup flour
- 1 stick butter, sliced thin
- ¼ cup cheddar cheese, grated

Place apples in buttered casserole dish. Mix water cinnamon, and lemon juice; pour over apples. Mix flour, sugar, butter, and cheese. Spread over top. Bake at 350 degrees for 1 ½ hours. Serve hot with vanilla ice cream.

① Swordfish

essense

Olive Oil

② Cover
1) Onion + Olive Oil
2) Garlic
3) tomato
4) white wine
5) 2 kind of olive oils

Apple Strudel

- 6 layers Phyllo dough
- ¼ cup brown sugar
- ½ cup butter, melted
- 1 tsp cinnamon
- 3 large Granny Smith apple, peeled, cored and diced
- 2 tbs sugar
- ½ tsp cinnamon
- ½ cup raisin

Preheat oven 350 degrees. Place first layer of Phyllo dough cookie sheet. Brush layer with butter. Repeat with each layer. In a bowl combine apples, raisins, brown sugar and cinnamon. Spoon filling down the left side of dough. Fold top edge and bottom edge about 2" to cover filling. In small bowl mix sugar and cinnamon, set aside. Roll dough over to enclose filling (it will look like a log). Brush with remaining butter and sprinkle with cinnamon sugar. Bake for 30 minutes or until golden brown and puffed.

① Bacon oil remaing +
Brown sugar +   dressing
vinegar   for salad

+

Salad + egg + salt + pepper
Apple graded to the core

DI

TOSS IT
+ Fried potatoes and season with salt
Add

Baked Sliced Apples

- 4 large apple –(McIntosh), sliced ¼ inch thick
- 3 tbs lemon juice
- ¼ cup light brown sugar, packed
- ¼ cup unsalted butter, cut in ½ inch cubes
- 2 tbs rum
- 4 3inch cinnamon sticks
- mint leaves (optional for garnish)

Preheat oven to 450 degrees. Peel and core apples, leaving them whole.
Slice apples in 1/4" slices. Reassemble the apples to form a whole apple.
Brush the apples with lemon juice. Place apples in pie plate or other baking
vessel. Fill the center with brown sugar, butter and rum. Sprinkle the
remaining brown sugar, butter, and rum.

Bake for 25 minutes. Reduce heat to 350 degrees and place one cinnamon
Stick in each apple and bake for 20 more minutes or until they are tender and
brown and the juices are thick and syrupy. Basting the apples frequently.
Place apple on serving plate, spoon syrup over the apples and garnish with
mint leave.

Pumpkin Mousse with Drunken Apricots

Darn those apricots! You can't take them anywhere.

- 3/4 cup dried apricots
- 4 tbs rum
- 16 oz unsweetened pumpkin filling
- 1 cup brown sugar
- 4 tbs butter, melted
- 1/2 cup pecan, chopped
- 1/4 tsp ground nutmeg
- 1/4 tsp ground cinnamon
- 1/4 tsp allspice
- 1 cup heavy whipping cream

In a saucepan, bring apricots and rum to a boil. Reduce heat and simmer for 1 minute. Take off heat and cool. When the apricots are cool enough to handle, dice them up into small chunks.

In a large bowl, mix together pumpkin, brown sugar, butter and spices. Then, add apricots and nuts, mix well.

In a mixer, whip cream until stiff peaks start to form (do not over whip). Fold 1/2 of the whipped cream into pumpkin mixture, once folded add remaining 1/2 and fold. For presentation, spoon mousse into 6 ounce wine goblets, top with whip cream. Sprinkle cinnamon sugar and garnish with rolled cookie.

Strawberry Margarita Mousse

- 4 cups whole strawberries, hulled
- 1 cup sugar
- 3 tbs boiling water
- 4 tsp unflavored gelatin
- ¼ cup tequila
- 1 tbs triple sec, or other orange-flavored liqueur
- 2 cups plain nonfat yogurt

Process strawberries in a blender until smooth. Pour into a large bowl; stir in sugar. Cover and let stand 30 minutes, stirring occasionally. Combine boiling water and gelatin in a small bowl; let stand 5 minutes or until gelatin dissolves, stirring constantly. Add the tequila and triple sec, and stir well. Stir the gelatin mixture into the strawberry mixture.

Cover and chill for 10 minutes or until the mixture begins to thicken. Add yogurt (at room temperature), stirring with a wire whisk until well-blended. Divide the mixture evenly among 5 margarita glasses or large stemmed glasses; cover and chill at least 4 hours or until set.

Strawberry Shortcake with White Chocolate

<u>Cake</u>
- 2 1/3 cups Bisquick
- ½ cup of milk
- 3 tbs sugar
- 3 tbs butter, melted
- 6 oz mini semi sweet chocolate morsels

<u>Topping</u>
- 1 pint baskets strawberries, hulled and quartered
- ¼ cup sugar
- 1tbs Grand Marnier or other orange liqueur

<u>White Chocolate Mousse</u>
- 8 oz good quality white chocolate (such as Baker's), finely chopped
- 1 2/3 cups whipping cream, chilled

For the shortcakes, preheat the oven 425 degrees. Mix the first 4 ingredients together, and then add chocolate morsels to dough. Place 6 spoonfuls onto a cookie sheet (this should use up all the dough). Bake 10 - 12 minutes or until brown.

For the topping, toss strawberries, sugar and liqueur in a large bowl. Let stand at room temperature until juices form, tossing occasionally, about 1 hour.

The mousse, melt chocolate and 2/3 cup of cream in a heavy medium saucepan under low heat. Transfer chocolate into large bowl. Let stand until mixture is cool and beginning to thicken, stirring occasionally, about 30 minutes. Beat remaining cream in medium bowl until stiff peaks form. Fold into chocolate mixture in 2 additions. Cover and chill at least 2 hours (can be made a day ahead.) Keep chilled.

Cut shortcake in half horizontally. Place bottom half on plate. Spoon 1/3 cup of mousse on shortcake. Then spoon strawberries on top of mousse. Then place remaining half of shortcake on top. Top with a spoonful of mousse and more strawberries and serve.

Berries with Chocolate Sauce

- 4 slices of angel food cake
- 2 pints strawberries, rinsed, hulled and cut in half
- 1 pint raspberries, rinsed and dried
- 2 tbs sugar
- ¼ cup of dark rum (more if you like)
- ¾ cup water
- 4 oz semi sweet chocolate morsels
- 2 tbs heavy cream
- 1 tbs butter

Preheat the oven 475 degrees. Set angel food cake slices on a baking sheet and toast in oven to make less spongy. Rinse and hull strawberries and cut them in half. Rinse and dry raspberries.

Over double boiler, melt butter with chocolate morsels. Stir in sugar until it dissolves. Add heavy cream, followed by water, stir until desired consistency. Stir in rum.

Place toasted cake on plate, top with fruit, followed by chocolate sauce.

Dessert Crepes

- 2 eggs
- 1/3 cup milk
- 1/3 cup water
- 3 tbs Grand Marnier (any liqueur will do)
- 3/4 cup flour
- 1 tbs melted butter
- 2 tbs sugar

Whisk together eggs, milk and water until combined. Gradually add the flour, whisking constantly until mixture is smooth.   Add the liqueur and the butter and whisk again. Very Important! Place a strainer over bowl and pour batter through strainer. This make sure the batter is smooth.

Preheat a 6" to 8" skillet on medium heat. Pour just enough batter to thinly cover the bottom of the skillet. Cook until bubbles start to form, then flip. Use wax paper in between each crepe to keep them from sticking together. Place crepe on plate, fill center of crepe with pie filling. Take one side of crepe and fold to center, then take other side and fold to center. Flip crepe over.

Preheat oven to 350 F and heat crepes for about 10 minutes. Top with whipped cream and more of the filling. You can also used these crepe cold, fill them with ice cream and top with your favorite chocolate or fruit sauce.

Crepes with Apple and Carmel

Crepes

- 2 eggs
- 1 cup milk
- 1 cup flour
- 1 tsp salt
- 1 tbs butter, melted and cooled

Beat eggs with whisk in medium bowl. Wisk in milk. Slowly whisk in flour and salt. Stir in butter. Heat in an 8 inch non-stick skillet over medium heat. Pour enough batter to thinly cover skillet. Turn when edges are dry and come loose.

Apple Filling

- 2 – 3 Granny Smith apples, peeled and sliced
- 1 tbs butter
- 3 tbs brown sugar
- ½ tsp cinnamon
- ¼ seedless raisins
- caramel sauce

Heat skillet to medium heat. Melt butter. Stir in sugar and cinnamon. Add apples and cook about 10 minutes, or until apples are soft. Add raisins. Place on cooked crepe. Roll and top with caramel sauce.

Cold Strawberry Soup

- 16 oz strawberries (frozen or fresh)
- 1 cup buttermilk
- ½ cup sugar
- 1 cup sour cream
- 2 tbs strawberry liqueur

Place all ingredients into a food processor or blender. Mix until strawberries are finely chopped. If you are using fresh strawberries, you may have to refrigerate e the soup for a couple of hours. Pour soup in a small bowl and place a spoonful of sour cream in the middle.

Giant Chocolate-Toffee Cookies

These cookies are great with coffee, better with a glass of Cabernet, even better with an ice-cold glass of milk! There's some work involved, but well worth the effort.

- ½ cup all purpose flour
- 1 tsp baking powder
- ¼ tsp salt
- 16 oz. semisweet chocolate, chopped up (don't use chocolate chips)
- ¼ cup unsalted butter
- 1 ¾ cup brown sugar, packed
- 4 large eggs
- 1 tbs vanilla
- 4 oz Heath bars, chopped
- 1 cup pecans, toasted and chopped

Combine flour, baking powder and salt in small bowl; whisk to blend. Stir chocolate and butter in the top of a double boiler set over simmering water until melted and smooth. Remove from over water and cool to lukewarm.

In your mixer, beat sugar and eggs until thick, about 5 minutes. Beat in chocolate mixture and vanilla. Stir in flour mixture, then toffee and nuts. Chill batter for 45 minutes.

Preheat oven to 350 degrees. Line cookie sheet with Parchment paper (wax paper will be okay). Drop 1/4 cup of batter onto cookie sheet, spacing 2 1/2" apart (cook 6 cookies at a time). Bake until top of cookie starts to crack; about 15 minutes (do not over bake). Cool cookies on cookie sheet. Make sure the cookie is cooled almost all the way or it may stick to the paper.

Peanut Butter and Milk Chocolate Cookies

- ¼ cup butter
- 1 cup *Jif* brand peanut butter
- ½ cup granulated sugar
- ½ cup brown sugar
- 1 egg
- ½ tsp vanilla
- ½ tsp salt
- ½ tsp baking soda
- 1 cup flour
- 6 regular sized *Reeses* peanut butter cups (broken in small pieces)

Preheat oven to 350 degrees. Cream butter and peanut butter in bowl. Beat in sugars. Add egg and vanilla then beat well. In another bowl mix salt, baking soda, and flour together then add to other mixture, mix well. Add broken peanut butter cup pieces. Form pieces using a tablespoon and place on greased cookie sheet. Press each down with fork (crossways). Bake 7-10 minutes on upper rack of oven (so bottoms of cookies don't burn).

Chocolate Chip Meringues with Berries

- 1 large egg white
- 1/8 tsp cream of tartar
- dash salt
- ¼ cup powdered sugar
- 1 tbs semisweet chocolate chips
- ¼ tsp vanilla extract
- ½ cup berries (choice in up to you)
- ½ tsp sugar
- 1 tbs Chambord (rum can also be used)

Preheat oven to 250 degrees. On a baking sheet, place a sheet of parchment paper and draw two 3" circles about 2" away from each other. Flip paper over and secure it onto the pan with masking tape.

Beat egg white, cream of tartar and salt on high speed until foamy. Add powdered sugar 1 tablespoon at a time, beating until stiff peaks form. Do not under beat. Fold in chocolate chips and vanilla. Divide egg mixture evenly between two circles. With the back of a spoon, shape meringues into nest. Bake for 1 to 1 ½ hours or until dry. Turn off oven and cool meringues in a closed oven for at least 3 hours. Carefully remove meringues from paper and place on serving plate.

Combine berries, sugar and liquor and spoon berries over the meringues and serve.

Fudgy Wudgy Brownies

This is the recipe that started it all for Dan. If you love chocolate and caramel this is your brownie. It is very rich, so a little goes a long way. At Dan's house, they just leave a knife in the pan and cut off a little at a time.

- 2 boxes German Chocolate cake mix
- 1 12oz can evaporated milk
- 12 oz semisweet chocolate chips (or more)
- 12 oz caramel candy (or more), melted
- 1 cup butter, melted

Preheat Oven to 350. Melt caramel & 1/3 can of evaporated milk until smooth using a double boiler over medium heat (You can use the microwave, about 6-8 minutes of power 5). Using a large bowl, mix Cake mix, butter and remaining evaporated milk with a fork (don't use the mixer; it's not worth the clean up). Batter will be very thick.

Using a 13 x 9 x 2 cake pan (no need to grease), take about 1/3 of the batter and smooth over the bottom of the pan (use your hands it's easier). Bake for 8 minutes or until cake is starting to rise. Remove from oven. Pour Chocolate chips over hot batter. Let sit for 6 minutes. Take the caramel mixer and pour over chocolate chips. With the remaining batter, take small amounts and make little patties and place on top until fully covered. The patties do not have to be flat. Use all the batter. Bake for 25 to 30 minutes. Cool and Eat!

Serving Ideas: If you have an incredible sweet tooth, place a scoop of French Vanilla ice cream on top of the brownie and then pour hot fudge on top of everything.

Mocha Java Trifle

- 1 angle food cake
- 1 large package instant chocolate fudge pudding
- Kahlua liqueur
- 1 pint whipping cream
- 4 tbs powder sugar
- 4 ripe bananas
- 1 large chocolate bar, frozen

Make pudding and set aside. Whip cream and sugar together until stiff.
Break cake into pieces, place half in bottom of trifle dish. Sprinkle Kahlua
over cake. Top with half of pudding followed by half cream. Repeat layer.
Grate frozen chocolate to top.

Brownie Berry Torte

- 1 box brownie mix
- 3 large eggs
- ½ cup oil
- ½ cup water
- 9 oz chocolate chip
- 1 tub Cool Whip
- 2 tbs orange liqueur
- 2 cups strawberries, sliced
- 2 tbs sugar
- 2 tbs orange liqueur
- 3 oz chocolate chip
- 2 tbs butter
- 2 tbs corn syrup, light

Preheat oven to 325 degrees. Prepare brownie using the directions on the box. Use 3 eggs and add chocolate chips to the batter. Using and 8x8 pan lined with parchment paper on the bottom. Bake brownies for about 50 minutes. Cool completely.

While brownies cool, slice strawberries and mix with sugar and liqueur. Let stand. Fold in orange liqueur into Cool Whip. Refrigerate. Melt together 3 ounces chocolate chips, butter and corn syrup until smooth. Set aside. Take brownie out of pan and place on serving dish. Spread cool whip mixture on brownie. Place strawberries slices on cool whip. Drizzle chocolate sauce over entire torte.

Banana Cream Torte

- 1 pint of whipping cream, whipped
- 1 package vanilla pudding mix
- 1 can sweetened condensed milk
- 5 cups ice cold water
- vanilla wafer cookies
- 4 bananas, peeled and sliced

Mix the dry pudding mix with the condensed milk and water. Stir, then let sit until thicken (about 5 minutes). Add whipped cream. Layer in this order: cookies, bananas, pudding/cream mixture.

Lemon Cheesecake Bars

You can't live in southern California without enjoying these bars each year. There seems to be a law mandating that people with lemon trees make these bars for everybody.

Crust

- 2 cups flour
- ½ cup powder sugar
- 1 cup butter, soften

Filling

- 8 oz cream cheese, soften
- 2 eggs
- 2/3 cup evaporated milk
- ½ sugar
- 1 tbs flour
- 1 tbs lemon juice

Topping

- 1 cup sour cream

Preheat oven to 350 degrees. For the crust, in a medium size bowl, mix flour and powder sugar. Cut butter into flour mixture until crumbly. Press mixture into bottom of a 13x9x2 pan, and up sides 1 inch. Bake for 25 minutes. Cool on rack.

For the filling, mix together, cream cheese, eggs, milk, sugar, flour, lemon juice and lemon peel. Mix until smooth. Pour into partially baked crust and bake for additional 15 minutes or until set. Cool completely. Once cool, spread sour cream over the top and refrigerate. Cut into 1 inch by 2 inch bars.

Blueberry Cheesecake Squares

- 1 package blueberry muffin mix
- ½ cup butter, softened
- 8 oz. cream cheese, softened
- ½ cup sugar
- 1 egg
- 3 tbs lemon juice
- 1 tsp grated lemon peel

Preheat oven to 350 degrees. Pour muffin mix in bowl, cut in butter. Press into bottom of baking pan. Bake for 15 minutes.

Combine cream cheese and sugar in medium bowl. Beat until smooth. Add egg, lemon juice, lemon peel. Beat well. Spread over baked crust. Return to oven for 35 - 40 minutes (or until filling is set). Cool completely then chill until ready to serve. Cut into squares.

Coconut Chocolate Bars

- 1 package chocolate cake mix
- 1/3 cup butter
- 1 large egg, slightly beaten
- 14 oz can sweetened condensed milk
- 1 large egg
- 1 tsp vanilla extract
- 1.5 cups sweetened coconut
- 1 cup pecans, chopped
- 1 cup chocolate chips

Preheat oven to 350 degrees. Combine cake mix, butter, and slightly beaten egg in large bowl. Mix with fork until crumbly. Press into bottom of ungreased 13 x 9" baking pan.

Combine sweetened condensed milk, egg, and vanilla extract in medium bowl. Beat for 3 minutes. Stir in 1 cup of the coconut, pecans, and chocolate chips. Spread evenly over cake mixture. Sprinkle with remaining coconut. Bake for 25 – 30 minutes on center rack of oven. Remove and cool in pan on wire rack.

Mini Cheesecakes

A great recipe for the kids because they are simple to make and taste great. You can use different cookies for the crust. Add chocolate chips or fruit to the batter.

- 1 package Vanilla Wafers
- 16 oz cream cheese, room temperature
- ¾ cup sugar
- 2 eggs
- 1 tsp. vanilla

Line muffin tin with cupcake liners. Place one vanilla wafer in the bottom of each liner. Cream together cream cheese, sugar, eggs and vanilla. Fill each cupcake liner ¾ full (do not over fill). Bake 15 minutes at 375 degrees. Makes about 12-14

Chocolate Pecan Pie

- 4 oz semisweet chocolate
- 2 tbs butter
- 3 large eggs
- 1/3 cup sugar
- 1 cup corn syrup (light & dark)
- 1 tsp vanilla extract
- 1 ¼ cups pecan halves
- 1 unbaked 9" pie shell

Preheat oven to 350 degrees. Melt chocolate and butter in double boiler. Microwave can be used at 30 second increments at medium power until melted. Cool slightly. Beat eggs lightly in medium bowl. Add sugar, corn syrup, chocolate mixture and vanilla. Stir until well blended. Stir in pecans.

Place pie shell on heavy cookie sheet and pour in filling. Spread filling until even. Bake for 50-55 minutes or until knife comes out clean. Cool on wire rack to room temperature.

California Lime Pie

Don't waste precious time searching for Florida Key limes (even though they're more intense in flavor than California limes) use the limes that are so abundant here!

- 6 oz cream cheese, softened
- ¼ cup real butter, softened
- 14 oz sweetened, condensed milk
- 1/3 cup lime juice
- 1 ready-made graham cracker pie shell
- lime slices, whipped cream

Cream butter and cream cheese together until fluffy. Add milk and lime juice, mix well. Pour into pie shell and cover with plastic wrap. Refrigerate 4 hours. Garnish with lime slices and whipped cream.

Goldfish Jell-O

Let the kids prepare this one.

- 1 package Jell-O instant gelatin mix (blueberry, lime, or other light color)
- 1 cup Pepperidge Farm (or other brand) goldfish crackers
- ½ cup small marshmallows

Prepare Jell-O per package instructions. Stir in goldfish and marshmallows as Jell-O is hardening (to minimize cracker sogginess). Serve when done.

Rum-Apple Bread

- ¼ cup butter, softened
- 1 cup brown sugar, firmly packed
- 3 large eggs
- ¼ cup dark rum
- 1 ¾ cups all-purpose flour
- 1 tsp baking powder
- ½ tsp baking soda
- ½ tsp salt
- 1 cup Granny Smith apples (2), peeled, and coarsely shredded
- ½ cup raisins
- ¼ cup walnuts (pecans can also be used), chopped
- vegetable cooking spray

Preheat oven to 350 degrees. Cream butter, and gradually add the sugar, beating at medium speed of a mixer until light and fluffy (about 5 minutes). Add eggs and beat until well-blended. Add rum; beat well.

In a small bowl, combine flour, baking powder, baking soda and salt. Add to creamed mixture; beat well. Stir in shredded apple, raisins and walnuts. Pour batter into a 9 x 5-inch loaf pan coated with cooking spray. Bake for 1 hour or until a wooden pick inserted in the center comes out clean. Let cool in pan 10 minutes on a wire rack; remove from pan, and let cool completely on wire rack. Serve with whipped cream or vanilla ice cream with a splash of rum over the top.

Kentucky Spiced Stack Cake

Dan takes a lot of ribbing because he uses so much booze in his recipes. But he never appears concerned, because in most of his recipes the alcohol cooks out. However, in this recipe the bourbon does not cook out, so don't eat and drive!

Spice Cake recipe

- 1 package Spice cake mix
- 3 large eggs
- 1/3 cup canola oil
- 1 1/3 cups water

Filling

- 3 ¼ cups water
- ½ cup brown sugar, packed
- ¼ cup bourbon
- 12 oz dried apples
- 1 tsp vanilla
- powdered sugar

Preheat oven to 350 degrees. Combine cake mix, eggs, water and oil in mixer. One minute on low speed and then two minutes at medium high. Pour batter into greased 12 cup bundt pan and bake for 40 minutes or until a wooden tooth pick comes out clean. Cool in pan for 10 minutes and then invert cake onto wire rack. Cool Completely.

While cake is cooling, prepare the filling. Combine all filling ingredients in a large saucepan and bring to a boil. Cover, reduce heat and simmer for 35 minutes or until liquid is nearly absorbed. Place apple mixture in a food processor, pulse 8 or 9 times until filling is a chunky puree. Set aside.

Slice cake horizontally into thirds using a serrated knife (fishing line works very well, too). Place bottom layer on serving plate. Spread half the apple filling over first layer. Take the middle layer and place on top of filling. Spread remaining filling and top with last layer of cake.

279

White Chocolate Chip Pumpkin Cake

<u>Spice Cake Recipe</u>

- 1 package spice cake mix
- 3 large eggs
- 1 cup canned pumpkin
- 2/3 cup evaporated milk
- 1 cup white chocolate chips
- 1/3 cup canola oil

<u>White Chocolate Glaze Recipe</u>

- 3 tbs evaporated milk
- 1 cup white chocolate chips
- ½ tsp ground cinnamon

Preheat oven to 350 degrees. Grease and flour 12 cup bundt pan. Combine cake mix, eggs, pumpkin, milk and oil in a large bowl. Beat at low speed until moistened. Stir in white chocolate chips. Pour into bundt pan and bake for 40 -45 minutes or until wooden tooth pick comes out clean. Cool on wire rack for 25 minutes, then invert onto wire rack to cool completely.

While cake is cooling, in a small sauce pan, bring milk to a slight boil. Remove from heat. Add white chocolate chips and stir until smooth. Stir in cinnamon. Drizzle over cake.

Cranberry Upside-Down Cake

- 1 cup sugar
- 2 large eggs yolks (save the whites!)
- 1 ½ tsp vanilla
- 6 oz sweet butter, softened
- 3/4 cup light brown sugar
- 24 oz fresh cranberries, rinsed and drained
- ½ cup milk
- 2 large egg white (I told you to save them)
- 2 tsp baking powder
- 1/4 tsp salt

In a 9" spring form pan, melt brown sugar with 2 ounces of butter. Stir constantly until sugar is completely dissolved. Pour cranberries onto brown sugar mixture. Set aside.

In another bowl, cream the remanding butter with sugar until smooth. Stir in egg yolks and vanilla.

In a large bowl combine flour, baking powder and salt. Alternately mix the milk and sugar mixture into dry mixture.

Beat egg whites until stiff peaks form, and then fold into cake mixture. Mixture will be thick. Pour over cranberries, spreading batter evenly. Don't worry about getting the batter down into the cranberries, it will work it way down while it is baking. Bake at 350 degrees for 50 - 60 minutes or until cake is done. Cool Completely.

Take out of spring form pan. Place piece of cake on plate and top with whip cream, cranberries and a mint leaf.

Caramelized Apple Upside-down Cake

- 1 tbs unsalted butter
- ½ cup light brown sugar, firmly packed
- ¼ tsp cinnamon
- dash nutmeg
- small apples, thinly sliced

Cake

- 6 tbs unsalted butter, soften
- 1 cup sugar
- 2 eggs, room temperature
- 1 tsp vanilla extract
- 1 cup flour
- 1 tbs cornmeal
- 1 tsp baking powder
- ½ tsp salt
- ½ cup milk

Preheat over to 350 degrees. Lightly butter the sides of a 9 inch cake pan. Combine the butter, sugar, cinnamon and nutmeg in a small saucepan. Boil for 30 seconds. Pour mixture into cake pan and spread evenly. Place apples all over and press down slightly in mixture.

To make the cake, beat the butter and sugar in a mixer until creamy. Add eggs and vanilla and beat until very smooth and fluffy. Sprinkle in flour, cornmeal, baking powder and salt. Beat 10 seconds. Pour in the milk and beat until the batter is evenly moistened. Spoon the batter over the apples and smooth the top.

Bake 50 minutes, or until done. Run a knife around the outer edge of the cake to loosen. Place a plate over the cake, and then flip it over to invert the cake onto the plate. Let the cake cool completely before serving

Lemon Gingerbread Cake with Lemon Glaze

- 2 tbs sugar
- 2 tbs margarine, softened
- 2 tsp lemon rind, grated
- 1 egg white
- ½ cup nonfat buttermilk
- ½ cup molasses
- 1 cup all-purpose flour
- ½ cup whole-wheat flour
- ½ tsp baking soda
- ¼ tsp salt
- ¼ tsp ground ginger
- ¼ tsp ground cinnamon
- vegetable cooking spray
- 2 tsp powdered sugar

Lemon Glaze

- ½ cup lemon juice
- ½ cup powdered sugar
- ½ tsp vanilla
- ½ tsp almond extract
- ½ tsp butter extract

Preheat oven to 350 degrees. Cream sugar and margarine at medium speed of an electric mixer until light and fluffy (about 5 minutes). Add lemon rind and egg white; beat at medium speed until well blended. Combine buttermilk and molasses; set aside. Combine all-purpose flour, whole-wheat flour, baking soda, salt, ginger, and cinnamon. With mixer running at low speed, add flour mixture to creamed mixture alternately with buttermilk mixture, beginning and ending with flour mixture.

Pour batter into an 8-inch square baking pan coated with cooking spray. Bake for 25 minutes or until a wooden pick inserted in center comes out clean. While cake in cooling, mix together all Glaze ingredients. Mixture will be thin. Take a tooth pick and stick it in and out of the cake. Using a pastry brush, paint glaze over cake. Let glaze harden and re-apply glaze.

Dump Cake

*Got a sudden sweet tooth? Feel like baking up something quick at
11:00 PM? Then here's a recipe for you.*

- 1 box yellow cake mix
- 1 can apple pie filling
- 1 cup butter, melted

Preheat oven to 350 degrees. Using a 13x9 pan, sprayed with cooking spray,
dump pie filling and spread across bottom of pan. Sprinkle dry cake mix
over pie filling. Drizzle butter over cake mix. Bake for 30 minutes or until
top is golden brown.

Coconut Cake

- 1 cup butter, softened
- 2 cups sugar
- 6 large eggs
- 2 cups flour, sifted
- 2 cups grated coconut
- 1 tbs vanilla

Preheat oven to 300 degrees. Cream butter and sugar until smooth. Add
eggs one at a time. Beat well after each egg. Add flour and stir until well
combined. Stir in coconut and vanilla. Pour batter into a prepared (greased
& parchment paper) 9" round cake pan. Bake for 1 hour. Reduce heat to
200 degrees and bake additional 20 minutes. Cool completely

Butterfinger Crumb Cake

- 2 cups flour
- 1 cup brown sugar, packed
- ½ cup sugar
- ½ butter
- ½ cup Butterfinger candy bar, finely chopped
- 1 tsp baking soda
- ½ salt
- ½ cup plain yogurt
- 1 egg
- 1 tsp vanilla

Grease 8 inch square baking pan combine flour, brown sugar and sugar in mixing bowl. Cut in butter until mixture is coarse crumbs. Transfer ½ of the mixture into other bowl. Stir in Butterfinger pieced, baking soda, salt and remaining flours mixture. Set aside.

In another bowl mix milk, yogurt, egg and vanilla until well blended. Add flour mixture and stir until blended, pour in pan and bake in over at 350 degrees for 40 - 45 min. Cool slightly and serve warm.

Three-Well Chocolate Cake

How did this cake get this name? By the way in which it's prepared. As fun to make as it is to eat!

- 1.5 cups sifted flour
- 1 tbs cocoa
- 1 tsp baking soda
- 1 cup sugar
- ½ tsp salt
- 3 tbs vegetable oil
- 1 tbs white vinegar
- 1 tsp vanilla
- 1 cup cold water

Preheat oven to 350 degrees. Grease 8-inch square baking pan. Resift flour along with cocoa, soda, sugar, and salt directly into the pan. Make three wells in the dry mixture. Fill one well with oil, second with vinegar, and third with vanilla. Pour cold water over all. Mix well with spoon. Bake for 30 minutes.

Double Chocolate Rum Cake with Raspberry Glaze

A Chocolate lover's delight. There's chocolate everywhere. The raspberry glaze is heavenly. It takes some time to create this masterpiece, but when you see the look on your guest's face after their first bite; it will truly be worth the time.

- 1 package chocolate cake mix
- 1 package chocolate pudding mix
- 4 large eggs
- 1 cup dark rum
- 3/4 cup water
- ½ cup canola oil
- 12 oz chocolate chips
- 10 oz raspberry preserves (seedless)
- 2 ½ tbs shortening
- 1 oz white chocolate

In a large bowl, combine cake mix, pudding mix, eggs, 1/2 cup of rum, water and oil. Mix for one minute on low speed, then 2 minutes on medium high. Once well combined, stir in one cup of chocolate chips. Pour into prepared bundt cake pan. Bake at 350 degrees for 50-60 minutes or until done.

Remove from oven, leave cake in pan for 15 minutes. Loosen sides, flip pan over on a wire rack and let the cake completely cool. Meanwhile, prepare the glaze. In a small saucepan mix the rest of the rum and raspberry preserves together. Bring to a slight boil over medium heat. Once you see bubbles starting to form, take off heat and let cool.

Poke several holes all over the cake using a fork. This will allow the glaze to seep into the cake. With a pastry brush, apply all the glaze over the entire cake (do not pour glaze over cake, brushing gives it an even coating).

Next, create the icing. Use a double boiler or microwave oven to melt 1cup of chocolate chips with 2 tbs shortening. While the icing is still warm, pour over the cake evenly. Let stand for 15 minutes (important).

After the dark chocolate icing has cooled completely, melt the white chocolate with ½ tablespoon of shortening. Drizzle over the cake. Let cool then serve.

Pumpkin Spice Cake with White Chocolate Glaze

- 1 package spice cake mix
- 3 large eggs
- 1 cup canned pumpkin
- 2/3 cup evaporated milk
- 1 cup white chocolate chips
- 1/3 cup canola oil

White Chocolate Glaze

- 3 tbs evaporated milk
- 1 cup white chocolate chips
- ½ tsp ground cinnamon

Preheat oven to 350 degrees. Grease and flour 12 cup bundt pan. Combine cake mix, eggs, pumpkin, milk and oil in a large bowl. Beat at low speed until moistened. Beat at medium speed for 2 minutes. Stir in white chocolate chips. Pour into bundt pan and bake for 40 -45 minutes or until wooden tooth pick comes out clean. Cool on wire rack for 25 minutes, then invert onto wire rack to cool completely. While cake is cooling, make glaze.

In a small sauce pan, bring milk to a slight boil. Remove from heat. Add white chocolate chips and stir until smooth. Stir in cinnamon. Drizzle over cake.

Apple-Pear Crisp

- ½ cup dried cherries
- 1/3 cup apricot preserves
- 1 tsp lemon peel – grated
- 2 tbs lemon juice
- 2 lbs pears – peeled, cored and sliced into ½ slices
- 1 lb Granny Smith Apples – peeled, cored and sliced into ½ slices
- 1 cup flour
- 1 tsp ground cinnamon
- ¼ tsp salt
- 6 tbs butter, chilled
- 1 cup oats – regular (not instant)
- ¾ cup raw sugar

Preheat oven to 375 degrees.

Combine the first six ingredients in a large bowl, tossing until everything is well coated. Pour into a 11 x 7 x 2 baking dish (coated with cooking spray). Set aside.

In a food processor, mix together flour, cinnamon, salt. Pulse 5 or 6 times. Add butter and pulse until mixture looks like course crumbles. Add oats and sugar; pulse 5 more times or until well combined.

Sprinkle dry mixture over fruit and bake for 1 hour or until top is golden brown and bubbly. Cool for about 10 minutes, serve warm or at room temperature over ice cream.

Banana Custard Pie with Chocolate Glaze

- Vanilla Wafer Pie Crust
- 2 large bananas

Custard

- 3 tbs.   cornstarch
- ¾ cups   sugar
- 1 ½ cup milk
- 1 lrg   egg (slightly beaten)
- 1 tsp.   butter extract

Glaze

- 1 tbs.   cocoa (unsweetened)
- 1 tbs.   butter (melted)
- 3 tbs.   powdered sugar
- 1 tbs.   hot water (if needed)

Preheat oven to 375 degrees. Bake crust for 5-7 minutes. Pull from oven and let cool. Slice bananas about ½ inch thick and cover the bottom of the crust. Set aside.

Prepare custard: combine cornstarch and sugar in a medium saucepan. Add milk slowly and heat, stirring constantly until mixture comes to a boil. Slowly add about ¾ cup of mixture to egg (continuing to stir). Stir back into the custard mixture, stirring for one more minute. Remove from heat and stir in butter extract and pour hot custard over bananas.

Prepare glaze: in a small bowl, mix cocoa, butter and powdered sugar until smooth. If mixture is too thick, add the water. Pour glaze over custard.

Refrigerate for several hours or overnight.

Easy Black & White Cookies

- Pre-made cookie dough (sugar or shortbread)

Chocolate Glaze

- ¼ cup cream
- 1 cup chocolate chips
- 2 tbs light corn syrup

White Chocolate Glaze

- ¼ cup heavy cream
- 1 cup white chocolate chips
- 2 tbs. light corn syrup

Preheat oven to 350 degrees.

On a floured breadboard, use a rolling pin to roll out dough until it is about 3/8" thick. With a cookie cutter (shape of your choice) cut dough and place on cookie sheet. Bake cookies 7-9 minutes or until bottoms start to brown. Let cool.

In a small saucepan, boil the milk until scalded (very hot), remove from heat. Add chocolate and corn syrup. Mix until smooth. Once smooth, let stand for 15 minutes. This will allow the mixture to cool down and thicken slightly. Repeat process with white chocolate.

Dip cookie into chocolate mixture. Covering half, or entire cookie (your choice). After you have dipped the cookies, place in refrigerator until hard (10 to 12 minutes). Repeat the dipping process with other chocolate mixture and refrigerate.

Easy Lava Cake

- 1 box Dark Chocolate cake mix
- 1 1/3 cup water
- ½ cup canola oil
- 3 eggs
- 1 cup chocolate chips
- 8 oz. dark chocolate - chopped
- 6 oz. heavy cream
- 4 oz. butter
- hot water
- whipped cream
- hot fudge

Preheat oven to 350 degrees.

Mix together cake mix, water, oil and eggs until well combined (do not over mix). Pour 2/3 of the batter into a prepared 12-cup Bundt pan. Sprinkle Chocolate chips on the batter. Top with remaining batter. Bake 40 to 45 minutes (don't over cook).

While cake is cooling, heat up cream and butter until a slight boil starts. Pour hot mixture on top of chopped chocolate and stir until creamy. Mixture (a.k.a. – Lava) should be thin. If too thick, add a little hot water,

Place a slice of cake on serving dish and pour lava over the top. Pour enough to pool around the slice. Top with whipped cream and drizzle with hot fudge.

Ice Cream Salsa

- 1 pint strawberries - hulled and coarsely chopped
- 1 cup pineapple – chopped
- ½ cup cucumber – coarsely chopped
- 1 tsp. lime peel – shredded
- 2 tbsp. lime juice
- ½ tsp. jalapeno – chopped
- 2 tbsp. honey
- ¼ tsp. black pepper

In a medium bowl, mix all ingredients until well combined. Cover and refrigerate for at least 2-3 hours or up to 24 hours.

Scoop Ice cream into a bowl, spoon salsa over the top and serve.

Cookies & Cream Torte

- Devils food Cake mix
- 1 1/3 cup water
- ½ cup canola oil
- 2 eggs
- 1 container frozen whipped topping, thawed
- 8 creamed filled chocolate sandwiches
- chocolate syrup

Preheat oven to 350 degrees.

Mix the cake mix, water, oil, and eggs until combined. Pour into a prepared 13" x 9" x 2" pan. Bake 30 to 35 minutes. Let cool.

Place cookies in a food processor and pulse until cookies are in small pieces. Fold cookies into whipped topping until well combined.

Cut cake in half cross-wise, then cut whole thing down middle (now have four pieces).

Place one piece of cake on your serving dish, spread some of the whipped topping over the top only. Place the second layer of cake on and top again. Place the third layer and top with the spread the remaining topping. Garnish with some more cookie chucks and a drizzle of chocolate syrup. Refrigerate until ready to serve.

Index

A

Albondigas Stew, 107
Antipasto Salsa and Chicken Wrap, 35
Apple Strudel, 255
Apple-Pear Crisp, 289
Arrabbiata Sauce, Shrimp with Feta, 239
Asparagus with Orange Butter Sauce, 134
Avgolemono Soup, 101

B

Baja Quiche, 14
Baked Beans, Better Than Ice Cream, 123
Baked Sliced Apples, 256
Balsamic Roasted Potatoes, 127
Balsamic Veggie Medley, 136
Banana Cream Torte, 270
Banana Pie with Chocolate Glaze, 290
Banana's Foster, 247
Barbecue Chicken Quesadilla, 41
Bean Tacos, mini, 52
Beef and Cabbage Rolls (Ramsa), 176
Beef Fajitas, New Mexico, 236
Beef Filets, Elegant, 232
Beef Stroganoff by Beverly Baker (Jeff's mom), 170
Beef Stroganoff by Sharon Underwood (Donna's mom), 170
Beef Tenderloin en Croute, 233
Beef, Crispy Orange, 229
Beer Boiled Shrimp, 50
Berries with Butterscotch-Amaretto Custard Sauce, 251
Berries with Chocolate Sauce, 260
Black Bean Salad in Bell Pepper Cups, 94
Blueberry Cheesecake Squares, 272
Blueberry Fool, 253
Bourbon Corn Chowder, 108
Brandied Blue Cheese, Walnut and Pear Toast, 65
Brie and Red Pepper Quiche, 30
Brownie Berry Torte, 269
Butterfinger Crumb Cake, 285

Index

C

Index

Index

F

Feta (Baked with Shrimp, 238
Feta Stuffed Chicken Breasts, 225
Fettuccini (Easy) in Clam sauce, 181
Fettuccini Alfredo, 205
Fettuccini with White Cheese and Asparagus, 206
French Bread with Green Onions and Cheddar, 117
French Bread, stuffed, 37
Fried Chicken Salad, 83
Fudgy Wudgy Brownies, 267

G

Garlic Lover's Refried White Beans, 128
Garlic Lover's Shrimp, 61, 222
Garlic Pesto Shrimp over Angel Hair pasta, 210
Garlic Roasted Asparagus with Parmesan, 133
Gingerbread Waffles with Fresh Berry Topping, 23
Goldfish Jell-O, 277
Green Beans and Tapenade, 133
Green Beans with Pecan Caramelized Onions, 132
Green Goddess Shrimp Salad, 85
Grilled Chicken with Strawberry-Kiwi Salsa, 217
Ground Beef and Cheese with Mushroom Casserole, 165

H

Hot and Sour Soup, 103, 192
Hot Artichoke Spread, 64
Hummus Dip, Fluffy, 54

I

Ice Cream Cookies, 249
Ice Cream Salsa, 293

J

Jalapeno Cornbread, 117
Jalapeños, grilled and stuffed with Sausage and Cheese, 51
Jalapenos, stuffed, Wally's, 52
Jicama Kiwi Salad, 82

Index

K

L

M

N

Index

O

Olive and Eggplant Tapenade by Dr. C, 53
Olive Lover's Steak, 234
Onion and Cheese Casserole, 122
Onion Lover Grilled Burgers, 174
Orange Beef Burritos, 199
Orange Bourbon Chicken, 223
Orange Chicken Sandwich, 31
Oyster Stew, Classic, 113
Oyster Stuffing, 121
Oysters, Greek Style Sautéed, 63

P

Pan Bagna, 40
Pasta Puttanesca – Harlot's Pasta, 211
Pasta Torta, 214
Peanut Butter and Maple French toast, 20
Peanut Butter and Milk Chocolate Cookies, 265
Pear, Cranberry & Pecan Salad, 79
Pear, Spiced Pecan, and Blue Cheese Salad, 78
Pears Flambé, 246
Pecan Waffles with Bananas, 24
Pecan-Cinnamon Monkey Bread, 25
Pepperoni Lover's Cheese Ball, 65
Pepperoni Pizza Chili, 188
Pineapple Chili Cheese Slaw, 90
Pizza Pot Pie, 187
Pizza Salad, 81
Pizza Spread, 66
Poppy seed Bread, 27
Portobello Mushrooms, stuffed, 43
Potato Cheese Pancakes, 120
Potato Frittata, 17
Prussian Omelet, 15
Puffy Cheese Rolls, 60
Pumpkin Mousse with Drunken Apricots, 257
Pumpkin Spice Cake with White Chocolate Glaze, 288

Index

R

S

Index